Exmoor
40 favourite walks

The author and publisher have made every effort to ensure that the information in this publication is accurate, and accept no responsibility whatsoever for any loss, injury or inconvenience experienced by any person or persons whilst using this book.

With special thanks to Will Wake for suggesting the Porlock to Nutscale Water walk.

published by
pocket mountains ltd
The Old Church, Annanside,
Moffat DG10 9HB

ISBN: 978-1-907025-907

Text and photography copyright © Richard Webber 2023

The right of Richard Webber to be identified as the Author of this work has been asserted by him in accordance with the Copyright, Designs and Patents Act 1988

A catalogue record for this book is available from the British Library

Contains Ordnance Survey data © Crown copyright and database 2023 supported by out of copyright mapping 1945-1961

All rights reserved. No part of this publication may be reproduced, stored in a retrieval system, or transmitted in any form or by any means, electronic or mechanical, including photocopying and recording, unless expressly permitted by Pocket Mountains Ltd.

Printed by J Thomson Colour Printers, Glasgow

Introduction

Straddling West Somerset and North Devon, Exmoor was designated a national park in 1954 and covers 693 sq km, making it one of Britain's smallest national parks. What it lacks in size, however, it makes up for in beauty and contrast as it contains some of England's most diverse landscapes, including moorland, farmland, woodland and coast.

Like Exmoor's fictional heroine Lorna Doone, it is both wild and gentle. It's easy to see why author R D Blackmore chose it as the setting for his novel about a family of outlaws expelled from Scotland who came south and terrorised the locals. The scenery stirs the imagination, thanks to the coastline of stark cliffs lining the Bristol Channel, the wooded valleys, tumbling streams and wild empty moors.

Fortunately, no large urban sites exist on Exmoor, with any settlements protected from commercial exploitation. The lush landscape – in places brushed by the influence of humans, other corners pure unbridled wilderness – is punctuated by quaint villages, small towns and farms.

The national park's rich green landscape, unlike other national parks, ends abruptly at its northern edge upon reaching precipitous cliffs. These high, rugged hog's-backed monsters have earned the coastline the accolade of possessing England's highest sea cliffs and, in places, the remotest, as in many spots there is no landward access for miles, thanks to the height and gradient of the cliffs.

Although Exmoor isn't without its bleak, harsh landscapes – as anyone who has walked along the remote bridleway on the high northwestern plateau known as The Chains in winter will testify – there is an overriding softness to this part of the world, exemplified by the smooth, gentle curves of the hills and the soothing whispers of the myriad streams making their way to the open sea.

Geology and climate

The majority of the rocks underlying Exmoor are from the Devonian period (around 416-359 million years ago) and they form three broad ridges running from east to west which have been cut by river valleys. The oldest rocks which make up the highest parts of Exmoor (Dunkery and The Chains massif, and Selworthy Beacon and Croydon Hill) are most resistant to erosion and weathering and can also be seen in the coastal cliffs of Hangman Hill and between The Foreland and Minehead. The younger rocks form a band of slates and sandstones to the south, running through Simonsbath, Exford and Wheddon Cross.

Many different processes have acted on the underlying rocks over millennia to create the landscape we see today, particularly erosion by water. During the last ice age (around 10,000 years ago), Exmoor had a peri-glacial climate. Crags, such as those seen at the Valley of Rocks, were formed through the process of frost-shattering, as were the scree slopes on the high moors and the broken coastal cliffs.

Pollen analysis shows that as the climate warmed, the landscape gradually became colonised by trees, including Scots pine, birch and hazel and then by oak, elm, alder and lime. It is likely that all of Exmoor was wooded until human clearance began around 4000BC. The surviving woodlands which cloak the steep valley sides and coastal valleys were managed for centuries as sources of wood for building, fuel, tools and charcoal.

Today they remain rich habitats supporting a wide range of mammals, birds and insects, as well as many rare plants which thrive in the clean air. On the woodland margins, red deer are perhaps the best known of the creatures that Exmoor's diverse landscapes support.

Exmoor's mild climate, with warm summers and cool winters, is influenced by altitude and by proximity to the sea. The uplands regularly receive more than 2000mm of rain per year (the UK average is around 900mm) and snow is not uncommon on high ground. The prevailing wind is from the southwest and while there is some shelter in the valleys, the moors are frequently very exposed to strong winds.

History

Hunter-gatherers in the late Mesolithic period (around 8000 years ago) were Exmoor's first inhabitants who exploited the woodlands and coastal plain (now under the Bristol Channel) for survival.

As people moved to a less nomadic existence, they formed settlements and there are 45 known prehistoric sites, dating from around 4000BC, on Exmoor; this is far more than are found in the rest of Somerset and Devon.

Exmoor is also known for many unusual stone settings (upright stones) dating from the Bronze Age and numerous burial mounds (barrows) survive, usually found on hilltop or ridge-top locations. In the Iron Age, defensive hillforts and other earthworks appeared in prominent sites, usually overlooking valleys, and the Romans also built fortlets and signal stations when they made it to Exmoor's coast.

In the medieval period, the warm climate suited the development of farming, with both livestock and crops grown, and villages and farms were established. Higher land was generally used for common grazing and a network of lanes and tracks developed which are still visible in today's landscape. The stone-faced banks topped with beech trees which are still prevalent on Exmoor marked the common grazing boundaries. The central part of Exmoor, however, was a royal hunting forest from Saxon times onwards and subject to Forest Law, so access was restricted and farming forbidden.

Farming on Exmoor took a big leap forward in the early 19th century when the industrialist John Knight bought the former royal forest. As well as draining and ploughing the land, he invested huge amounts of time, effort and hard cash building roads and canals. Although arable farming still proved very difficult to advance, Knight's investment in livestock paid off, particularly with sheep. Enclosure, housebuilding and the digging of drainage channels changed Exmoor, however, and many of the iconic features of the upland landscape, such as straight beech hedgebanks, can be attributed to the efforts of John Knight and his family.

Industry on Exmoor at this time mainly involved mining for iron and other ores, and several limekilns were established near the coast. Traces of the mineral extraction and workings can still be seen around the national park in the form of ruins and spoilheaps.

Recreational use of the landscape grew in popularity in the 19th century as trade and tourism took off with the expansion of the railway from Bristol to Taunton and Exeter in the 1840s. Further development of routes to the coast made it easier to access Exmoor and attitudes to the wild moorland scenery changed, largely thanks to the work of the wandering Romantic poets William Wordsworth and Samuel Taylor Coleridge and, of course, the novelist R D Blackmore. On the large estates, carriage rides and sporting activities became hugely popular and much money was invested in building bigger houses and establishing gardens full of specimen trees and plants. In the

20th century, the area continued to thrive as a tourist destination, particularly after Butlin's Holiday Camp was established at Minehead in 1962. Exmoor's latest important designation came in 2011 when it became Europe's first Dark Sky Reserve.

Rights of Way and navigation
There are around 1000km of public rights of way across the park, signified by the plethora of green-dashed lines weaving their way across the OS map in every conceivable direction. In this collection of walks, however, preference has been given to circular rather than linear routes, bar the walk along the South West Coast Path. This is largely due to the fact that public transport links across Exmoor are poor which means the starting points for the walks featured here are best reached by car. As well as classic walks for anyone visiting this region, such as the route up to Dunkery Beacon – the highest point not only on Exmoor but also in Somerset – there are several less-walked routes where you're unlikely to pass a soul. Many of the walks highlighted here can be completed within an hour, while others need a few hours or even half a day.

For each walk, a sketch map provides an overview of the route covered. However, these are not intended to be used for navigation. Instead, they simply provide a visual summary and should be used alongside an OS map when establishing the exact route to be walked. Virtually all of Exmoor is covered by just one map: Ordnance Survey's Explorer OL9. In fact, it is only the very tip of the southern border which slips onto another sheet – OS Explorer 114. The walks in this volume, with one exception, all feature on OL9.

Many people might have the pink OS Landranger map which, in its own right, is very useful. But with the scale of 1:50,000 (2cm to 1km) compared to the Explorer's 1:25,000 (4cm to 1km), the latter is far superior for walking purposes: it is more detailed, covers more paths and tracks and is easier to use while trekking across the moors and along the valleys.

The orange OS Explorer maps show the areas of open countryside and registered common land that have been categorised as Open Access Land. Such areas are marked on the sheet as a yellow wash and are unmistakable when the map is spread out in front of you.

It was the Countryside and Rights of Way Act 2000 which introduced such areas for England and Wales, providing sections of mountain, moor and heath where walkers are free to venture off the paths. Walkers had campaigned for decades for such rights and celebrated when more than 1.5 million hectares were opened up for people to enjoy.

It has to be pointed out, however, that people need to be responsible when venturing onto Open Access Land. Dog owners, for example, must keep their dogs on a short lead between 1 March and 31 July, the primary breeding period for ground-nesting birds, or at any time of year when near livestock.

Overall, there is excellent signage across Exmoor. Paths are not only generally well maintained, but signs are well placed and clearly marked; the National Park Authority does take particular care, however, in ensuring a balance is maintained between signage and the landscape. Signs are wooden and kept as small as possible in order to avoid detracting from the aesthetic beauty of the surroundings. Signs, waymarks and occasionally other objects, such as tree trunks, are colour-coded according to their classification. While public footpaths are yellow and public bridleways blue, restricted byways are purple and byways open to all traffic red.

Several long-distance walks cross Exmoor too, and some are recognised and signed accordingly. The South West Coast Path is indicated, like all National Trails, by an acorn symbol, the Tarka Trail a paw print, the Two Moors Way regional route by 'MW', the Coleridge Way regional route by a quill and the Macmillan Way by a 'MAC' symbol.

The myriad aspects of Exmoor's landscape are what make it such a special corner of England. Whether it's the wooded combes, deep valleys, open moorland or lush green fields, there's something for everyone. For many, however, the rugged coastline which forms the national park's northern boundary and stretches for around 55km, from Minehead in Somerset to Combe Martin in Devon, is a key draw.

This is the highest coastline in England, rising to around 433m at Culbone Hill while the country's highest sea cliff, at 244m, is found at Great Hangman, near the seaside town of Combe Martin. Facing north results in the cliffs avoiding the worst of the prevailing southwesterly winds and accounts for the abundance of coastal woodland.

Heading inland, Dunkery Hill is not only the highest point on Exmoor but also the whole of Somerset, and is crowned by a large stone beacon. This sandstone hill rises to around 519m and provides glorious panoramic views; it is estimated that on a clear day, hills as far away as 130km can be viewed.

Plenty of walking opportunities exist in this part of Exmoor, and picturesque Exford, at the heart of the national park, or Minehead, the gateway town to North Exmoor, are good places to base yourself while you explore the valleys and characterful villages of the area.

Brendon Common ▶

North Exmoor and Exford

1 Top of Porlock Hill 10
Start at the top of the hill and enjoy expansive sea views on this short walk

2 Robber's Bridge to Oare 12
Tour some of R D Blackmore's bandit country and visit a church which the author knew well

3 Yenworthy and Broomstreet 14
Samuel Taylor Coleridge found inspiration here and the landscape remains largely unchanged

4 Nutscale Water from Porlock 16
Enjoy a tour of moor and woodland that takes in a remote reservoir

5 Horner Wood 18
One of England's great oakwoods, home to a variety of wildlife

6 Countisbury to Porlock 20
Look up the bus timetable before setting off on this long coastal ramble

7 County Gate and Doone Valley 22
Go deep into the countryside to discover the Doone family hideout

8 Sister's Fountain 24
Make a pilgrimage to a peaceful spring and well and enjoy expansive coastal views on the way

9 South of Exford 26
Take to the moorland and cross tributaries of the River Exe to reach the old farm buildings at Lyncombe

10 Exford to Prescott 28
Enjoy a short stroll around the lush countryside north of the village at the very heart of Exmoor

11 Dunkery Beacon 30
Expansive views await at the summit of the highest point on Exmoor, a popular spot in the holiday season

Top of Porlock Hill

Distance 3.5km **Time** 1 hour
Terrain easy **Map** OS Explorer OL9
Access lay-by on the coastal side of the road after the cattle grid at the top of Porlock Hill

A notoriously steep section of the A39 climbs over Porlock Hill as it cuts across the top of Exmoor on its way to Lynmouth and beyond. Rising 400m in less than 3km, it is said to be the steepest A-road in England. This short walk starts at the top of the hill and visits the scenic toll road built by a local landowner as an easier alternative.

From the lay-by, turn left onto the road and head down Porlock Hill for around 100m, bearing right off the road at the public bridleway sign for Hawkcombe.

Follow the farm track, passing a barn on your right with fine views towards Dunkery Beacon on the left. You'll see Bromham Farm ahead in the distance as the track bends right.

Go through the gate alongside a cattle grid. After a few metres, look out for a small path on the right, signed for Whitstones. The path runs alongside the edge of ancient Hawkcombe Wood National Nature Reserve.

Eventually, you reach a wooden gate. Go through this and continue, with the trees soon replaced by heather and gorse and a deep wooded valley below on the left. The A39 can be seen ahead as you reach a grassy patch with holly and other

TOP OF PORLOCK HILL

stunted trees. Continue through the middle of the trees and at the signpost cross the A39 to follow the public footpath marked for the toll road.

Cross a car park and take the grassy path in the left-hand corner, looking out over the Bristol Channel and Hurlstone Point. At a split in the path go straight on, rather than veering left, to drop down through the heather.

Ultimately, you'll reach the tarmac toll road. Dating from the 1840s, it runs for just over 6km and is easier on the brakes than the A39. Dug out manually to give work to impoverished local people after the Napoleonic Wars, tolls were initially taken at the bottom of the hill by staff at The Ship Inn in Porlock. There is still a toll to pay today (for cyclists as well as cars), but it is well worth it for the wonderful elevated sea views.

Turn right and walk down the toll road. Where it bends left, you'll spot a track peeling off on the right, signposted as a public bridleway to Porlock Hill. Take this deeply-rutted track. Where it splits, go left and continue, ignoring the next grassy path on the right. You'll see a metal gate ahead. As you approach it, the track bends right and climbs briefly before returning to the lay-by at the start.

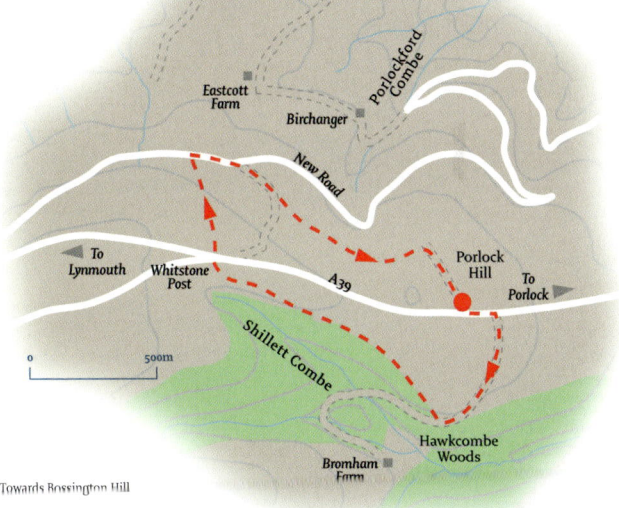

◀ Towards Bossington Hill

Robber's Bridge to Oare

Distance 9km **Time** 2 hours 30
Terrain sharp climbs both sides of the valley, and the final descent is relatively steep **Map** OS Explorer OL9
Access car park east of Robber's Bridge

Exmoor smuggling and banditry gave the Robber's Bridge over Weir Water its name and R D Blackmore the inspiration for his novel *Lorna Doone*. This walk starts at the old arch bridge and heads west before cutting up over fields to Stowey Ridge, then turning northwest down to Oare. Here, you'll find the famous church where Lorna Doone exchanged vows with John Ridd and was shot by the wicked Carver Doone. Spoiler alert – it's not fatal and John and Lorna live happily ever after.

From the car park to the east of Robber's Bridge, turn right and cross the bridge. Continue down the road, going over a second bridge just before the Old School House and another dwelling. Look for a wide path on the left, signed for Stowey Ridge and Larkbarrow. Pass through several gates, keeping straight ahead as you climb close to a field boundary.

After another gate, you'll face three tracks: choose the left option, continuing up over the field: this is Stowey Ridge.

Pass through several more gates until you reach a sign. Here, almost turn back on yourself towards Oare. Walk to another sign at the fence in the distance, right of a row of trees. Follow the bridleway sign.

Eventually, you pass through a gate with the blue bridleway marking. Carry on, now left of the boundary, going through two more gates and keeping straight ahead while admiring the view up over Cloud Allotment. Continue heading for Oare Church.

Walk past water troughs in the field and through a metal gate on the right. There is a sign left of the gate for Oare Church, but

◀ Turf Allotment

ignore this and head down the field, veering left to a bridleway sign and gate. Go through the gate and across another field, dropping into the far corner and up over a bank to a gate and sign. Continue to Oare, through the gate, keeping close to the fence on your left.

Follow the bridleway signs as you carry on downhill, passing the private garden of Oare Manor. At the end of the field, you arrive at a road: turn left onto this to reach Oare. R D Blackmore's grandfather had been the rector at St Mary's Church here and the author knew it well. Although the church is small, it would have been much smaller in the 17th century and the window through which the dastardly Carver Doone fired his pistol unglazed.

At the roadsign, turn right. After the bridge, turn right through a gate onto a footpath for North Common. Walk along the riverbank until a post indicates that all footpaths head left. Start to climb here. At a sign, go right for North Common. It is a hard slog now as you ascend the side of Deddy Combe.

Close to the top, a sign points to the left at a split but either route takes you to a gate at the top. Go through this and follow the signed footpath to North Common. This crosses tussocky grass as it runs to the left of the field boundary towards a small plantation.

Continue to the point where you see a stile by the trees near a bench. Don't cross the stile. Instead, turn right towards Oareford. The broad path bends across North Common. Where it splits, bear left, heading towards trees.

The path winds down to the river. At the valley bottom, go through a gate, cross a bridge and turn left to return to Robber's Bridge and the car park beyond.

Yenworthy and Broomstreet

Distance 5.5km **Time** 1 hour 30
Terrain easy going **Map** OS Explorer OL9
Access off-road parking on the A39 by the track leading to Yenworthy Lodge

This short walk in the northern reaches of the national park, just as it drops away to the Bristol Channel, has unbeatable views and an unlikely literary connection. It is thought that Samuel Taylor Coleridge wrote *Kubla Khan,* his 'vision in a dream', while staying at a farmhouse passed on the route.

Walk down the tarmac track, following the sign for County Gate. Pass the entrance to Yenworthy Lodge, heading in the direction of Yenworthy Farm.

At the next sign, turn right to a gate with a bridleway sign for Broomstreet. Go through this and keep the field boundary to your left. Further on, it turns sharp right. Continue, again keeping the boundary on your left as you walk through the large field to reach a gate with a blue bridleway marking.

Go through this, still keeping the original boundary to your left, and cross the field. The track drops down into a tiny valley and continues up the other side of the field. The route isn't clearly marked at this point so carry on across the field, keeping the boundary on your left.

Eventually, you'll reach a signpost in the corner of the field. Go through the gate on the left, heading for Broomstreet, and walk down over the field.

At a sign, close to the right-hand border, head for Porlock through the gate where a grassy path runs alongside a stone bank. You'll pass through a few gates.

YENWORTHY AND BROOMSTREET

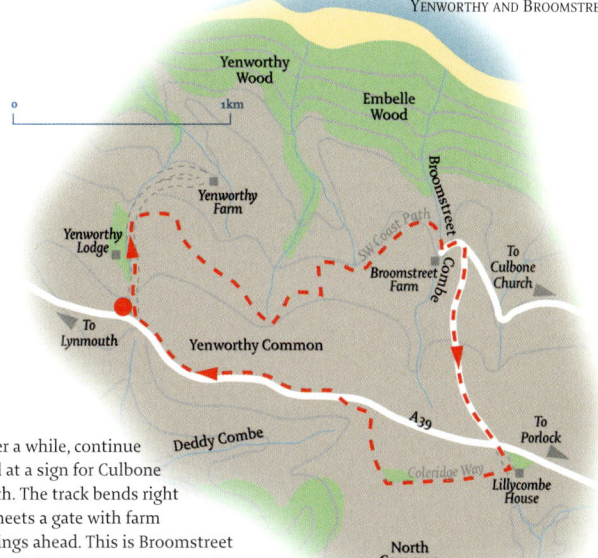

After a while, continue ahead at a sign for Culbone Church. The track bends right and meets a gate with farm buildings ahead. This is Broomstreet Farm and the farmhouse is said to be where Coleridge composed *Kubla Khan* one night in 1797 after waking from an opium-influenced dream about a Mongol Emperor. He had intended to write more than 54 lines but could not complete the work as he was interrupted by 'a person from Porlock' while writing it. Thus, 'a porlock' is an unwelcome intruder who disrupts inspired creativity.

Go through the gate, following the stony track until you come to a tarmac road. Turn left on this quiet road to Colbone Church and, as it bends around, continue at a sign in the direction of Oare before finally emerging at the A39. Cross this road and go over the stile at a footpath sign for Oare and Oareford. Walk down over the field.

Before reaching the boundary, turn right for Oare and Oareford, continuing to a stile in the corner. Beyond this, follow the path that runs next to a large clump of trees with a fence on your left.

At the corner of the tree plantation, go over the stile and turn immediately right for Yenworthy Common. Follow the track around to a gate. Go through this and back up to the A39. Initially, walk along the side of the road but look for a sign on the right, just a few strides away, marking a public bridleway for County Gate.

Go through the gate and walk across two fields, keeping close to the left-hand field boundary. Reaching the final boundary, pass through the gate to arrive at the start point.

◀ Storm approaching across the Channel

4 NORTH EXMOOR AND EXFORD

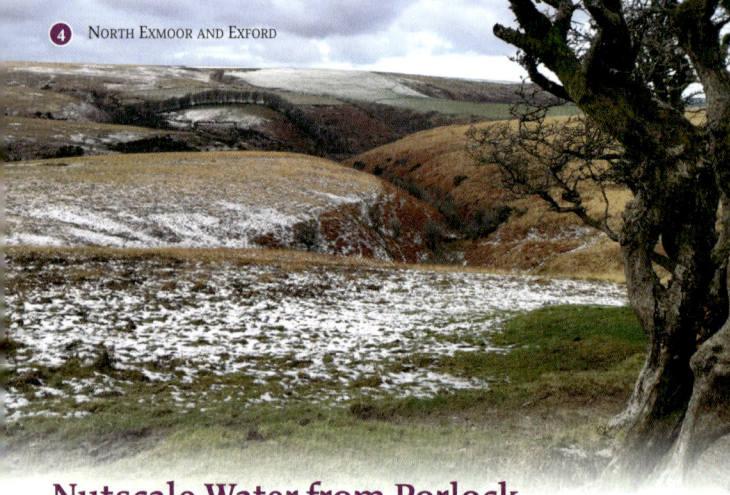

Nutscale Water from Porlock

Distance 15km **Time** 4 hours
Terrain some steep climbs and can be boggy in places; there are also streams to cross **Map** OS Explorer OL9
Access roadside parking on Porlock's Parsons Street

Beginning in the coastal village of Porlock, this longer route encompasses a varied landscape, including woods and open moorland, before following a stream in a deep valley which ultimately leads to Exmoor's most secluded reservoir. Look out for crowberry on the way; more common in upland Scotland, the plant only occurs in Southern England by Chetsford Water.

Walk up Parsons Street. At a no-through road sign, bear left before shortly joining the footpath for Lucott Farm, signed to the right of Glen Lodge at the bend.

The path climbs up through the woods. When it eventually drops down to a junction of paths, turn left to pick up the farm sign again and continue along the top edge of the wood.

Reaching a crossroads of paths, continue ahead. After around 500m, your route turns to go through a gate and up to Lucott Farm. At the farmhouse, turn right.

From here, walk along a track, up over fields and across Open Access Land in a southwesterly direction. After around 2km, look out for a yellow footpath arrow on a gatepost. Go through the gateway and carry on until you meet the road at Lucott Cross.

Turn left and either walk down the road for around 1km or alongside it until you reach a roadbridge. Turn left just before the bridge onto an unmarked path. Now it's a case of finding your way with

NUTSCALE WATER FROM PORLOCK

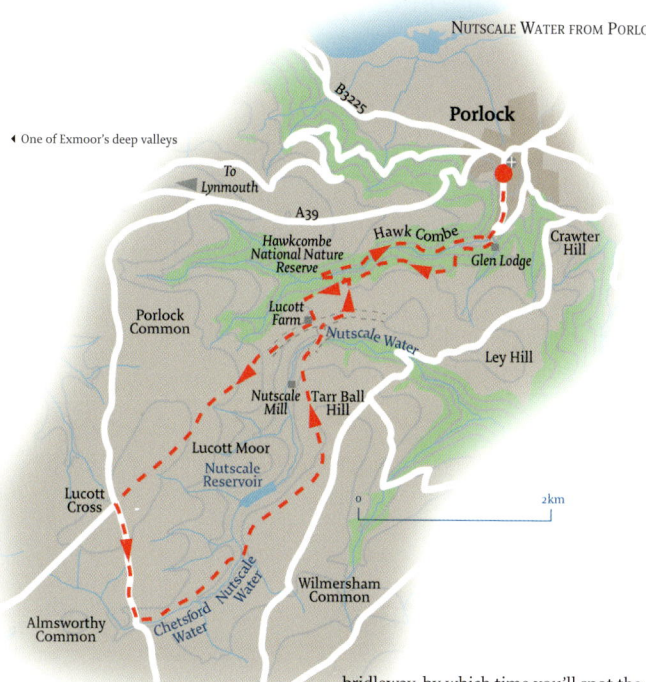

One of Exmoor's deep valleys

Chetsford Water, which later becomes Nutscale Water, on your right. You'll have to cross the stream when Chetsford is joined by Embercombe Water.

Follow the Nutscale in a northeasterly direction at Great Hill to pick up a clear track which climbs above Nutscale Reservoir. Built in 1942, it holds around 178 million litres and was designed to relieve summer droughts in Minehead.

Cross the reservoir's access road and walk across Tarr Ball Hill before dropping down past Tarr Ball Cottage on a bridleway, by which time you'll spot the Lucott Farm signs again.

After passing the cottage, the route crosses a footbridge, climbs back up to the farm and turns right, following the sign for Porlock via Hawkcombe. Head east along the farm lane, before soon turning left for Hawkcombe.

Cross two fields, go through a gate and walk down to the crossroads of paths you'll recognise from your outward journey. This time, head down into the combe. At the bottom, you have to cross Hawk Combe Water before turning right. Now, it's a case of walking back to Porlock.

Horner Wood

Distance 6km **Time** 2 hours
Terrain steep ascents and descents in places, particularly down through trees in Horner Wood **Map** OS Explorer OL9
Access National Trust car park in Horner

Horner Wood is one of Britain's largest ancient oak woodlands and is home to red deer, wood warblers, pied-flycatchers, lesser spotted woodpeckers, redstart and dipper, as well as 15 of the UK's 17 known bat species. Although it is a wild place today, the wood is the result of hundreds of years of intensive management, and prior to the early 20th century the trees here were regularly coppiced, pollarded, stripped of bark, burnt for charcoal or harvested for local housebuilding.

Turn left onto the lane from Horner's National Trust car park before shortly taking a path on the right marked as a public bridleway for Porlock and crossing a 17th-century packhorse bridge. The path bends right after the bridge. Look out for the next sign for Porlock, with the route now leading through the wood.

Go through a gate with an undulating path skirting around the back of Burrowhayes Farm, a caravan and campsite. Continue towards Porlock.

When the path splits, bear left, heading away from the fenced field boundary. Eventually, you'll see a narrow tarmac road on your right. Just before you arrive at the road, turn left up a path, signed as Granny's Ride, Horner Wood.

After a steady climb beyond the treeline, you emerge with fine views on your left, across fields to Periton Hill and Wootton Common, with Selworthy's unmistakable white church in view, too.

Ignore a path on your right and head

◄ Above Halse Combe

straight on. The path bends left, crosses a stream in the steep-sided Halse Combe and climbs to a sign, indicating three routes. Rather than continuing on Granny's Ride, take the right-hand route for Ley Hill, climbing uphill.

At a crossroads of paths, go straight on, as indicated by a blue arrow on a post. Remain on the main track, ignoring side routes.

Where the path splits by a post, keep right (ignoring the blue arrow pointing left). After a while, the wide path levels out. Keep straight on. As the path bends gently across the top of the hill, ignore any side routes. Where the path turns sharp right, bear left towards dense woodland.

The track enters Horner Wood. At a wooden sign, walk straight ahead. Almost immediately, the path splits – follow the middle option. At the next sign, with Granny's Ride signed left and right, continue straight downhill on an unmarked path. This is steep and uneven and can be slippery as it drops down through dense and moist woodland. It may feel more like a temperate rainforest here and some 330 species of lichen can be found clinging to the ancient oak pollards and fallen timber. Once a hive of activity, the woodland is now managed by the National Trust and is a protected National Nature Reserve.

You eventually exit the steep and wooded descent and meet a wide track. Turn left, with Horner Water running to your right. Continue back to Horner.

As you approach the village, go through a gate and over a stone bridge before turning left towards cottages, indicating you're arriving back in Horner.

Countisbury to Porlock

Distance 18km **Time** 5 hours (one way)
Terrain a few climbs and descents, but a relatively straightforward walk
Map OS Explorer OL9 **Access** Exmoor Coaster bus links Countisbury with Porlock for this linear walk

This walk on the South West Coast Path, England's longest waymarked trail, is a linear route so you'll need to buy a ticket for the coastal bus between Watchet and Lynmouth unless you want to start very early and retrace your steps. The route follows the acorn-emblazoned signs all the way to Porlock Weir, a small settlement around a harbour, and ends in the village of Porlock.

If arriving by bus, alight at Countisbury, just before Lynmouth. Opposite the Blue Ball Inn, follow the narrow road to the church and walk through the churchyard. Go through the gate behind the church and head for the fingerpost.

Here, you pick up the Coast Path, signed for Porlock, and the all-important acorn symbol signifying the South West Coast Path. The path winds its way around Foreland Point with spectacular views down the coast to Lynmouth.

You soon meet the access road to Foreland Lighthouse, which was first lit in 1900 and clings to the cliffs at Foreland Point, 67m above high tide level. This was always an unpopular posting for

◀ Wooded combes punctuate this stretch of coastline

lighthouse keepers as the steep north-facing slope only sees the sun for three months of the year.

Continue along the coast above the evocatively-named Desolation Point, through Glenthorne Plantation (part of the Glenthorne Estate, with its grand manor house and 4km-long drive) and past Sister's Fountain. Eventually, you enter Culbone Wood: largely comprising sessile oaks, it is one of England's longest stretches of coastal woodland.

The path reaches tiny Culbone Church, said to be the smallest parish church in England, which is situated in a deep wooded combe, before dropping down to Porlock Weir.

At this point, walk along the B3225, away from the weir, until you reach a fingerpost for the Coast Path to Bossington via the Marsh. The path skirts Porlock Marsh and passes a war memorial before crossing a wooden bridge. Soon after this, take a path on the right for Porlock which leads into Sparkhayes Lane and the village beyond.

The Exmoor Coaster's route runs from Watchet to Lynmouth, stopping at Blue Anchor, Dunster Steep, Minehead, Porlock and County Gate. So if you're based in Minehead, Watchet or elsewhere along this route, you can wait for the next bus to whisk you back to your base.

County Gate and Doone Valley

Distance 14.5km **Time** 4 hours
Terrain several ascents and descents
Map OS Explorer OL9 **Access** Exmoor Coaster bus to County Gate from Watchet, Minehead, Porlock and Lynmouth: car park at County Gate on the A39 near Lynmouth

Walk through a deep wooded valley and into the heart of *Lorna Doone* country to discover the now deserted and ruined Doone family homestead. Then rise up onto expansive Brendon Common, looking out for circling buzzards and red deer, before dropping into the pretty village of Brendon.

From the car park, head towards the main road before slipping through a gate on your right for Malmsmead. The path drops into a valley. At the bottom, bend right. Cross the footbridge at Oare Water and head to a gate. Trace the path by barns and through a gate marking the entrance to Parsonage Farm.

Reaching a road, turn right. Walk past Cloud Farm Campsite's entrance and over a stone bridge. Turn left on the signed lane leading to the public footpath for Doone Valley. You'll see a sign on a gate advertising a private footpath for a fee, but your route continues up the road.

After around 450m, take the wide track on your left, close to a bend. Head in the direction of Badgworthy Valley. The path turns to the left with the river on your left, too. When you're faced with two gates, pick the right-hand option and carry on. Ignore a footbridge on your left for Cloud Farm Campsite and a footpath to Oare Church. Walk straight on for Doone Valley. The path travels up the valley to the right of Badgworthy Water, passing a memorial stone dedicated to R D Blackmore, author of *Lorna Doone*.

Eventually, cross a footbridge as the route nears the head of the valley. At the confluence of rivers are the remains of the medieval village of Badgworthy, reputedly

County Gate and Doone Valley

◀ Leeford and Brendon

the inspiration for Blackmore's novel and the fictional home of the maverick Doone clan. The famous tale has some truth to it, however, as there was a real and very rebellious son of James Stewart, Lord Doune, who was exiled to Exmoor from Scotland in the early 17th century. By local accounts his clan was 'not peaceable' and returned north some years later.

At the crossroads of paths, head for Brendon Common. Soon, the path bends right, passing a blue-marked rock and post. The grassy path climbs onto the open common, passing a post with a blue arrow pointing straight ahead. At a split, keep right and go straight ahead at a fence and gate.

Here, a region inhabited by Exmoor ponies and red deer, you can see for miles. To your right, the view includes the Welsh coast and peaks of the Brecon Beacons.

The path sweeps around and descends to Lankcombe Ford before rising again (ignoring a path heading left) to Tippacott Ridge. At a signpost, go straight on for Brendon to reach a road. Cross, go over a cattle grid and head for Brendon at the Cross Gate sign. The road bends and descends steeply. Reaching Brendon, go straight across for Lynmouth, Lynton and Porlock. Once over the roadbridge, turn right for Porlock and walk up the road.

At Hall Farm, look for the footpath to County Gate. Climb the wooden steps and up the grassy field, where the path heads off to the left to a gate. Beyond is a short steep climb before the path drops, then passes through a gate and later a stepped stile. The route now traverses a field. Go through another gate, cross a footbridge and turn left uphill, before the path bends right to another gate. Continue following the path towards County Gate. The car park soon appears on the skyline.

Sister's Fountain

Distance 4.25km **Time** 1 hour 30
Terrain steep in places with uneven ground **Map** OS Explorer OL9
Access Exmoor Coaster bus to County Gate from Watchet, Minehead, Porlock and Lynmouth; car park at County Gate on the A39, near Lynmouth

Particularly colourful in summer when the rhododendrons are in bloom, this walk incorporates deep wooded combes, fine coastal views and the site of a Roman fortlet, as well as a spring reputed to have gushed forth from a spot made sacred when Jesus' uncle, Joseph of Arimathea, struck the ground with his staff.

If arriving by car, turn left at the car park entrance and walk along the road to pick up a route on the right, signed for Sister's Fountain, which drops to a large gate. Go through this for a steep descent on a path.

After ignoring a gate on your right, continue to another wooden gate. Go through this and turn right at the Seventhorns junction signpost, heading in the direction of the public footpath for the Coast Path and Glenthorne Beach.

A few metres down the track, turn left for the Coast Path and descend steps to reach the stone cross and pool of Sister's Fountain. In the 19th century, this natural spring was enclosed in stonework and given its name by the first owner of the Glenthorne Estate whose two nieces liked to play here. The local legend is that Jesus drank here as a child when he passed this spot with his uncle on the way to Glastonbury. It's not as implausible as it sounds as many of the first tin miners in England were Jewish settlers and it is thought that Joseph was a well-travelled tin trader.

From the fountain, head in the direction

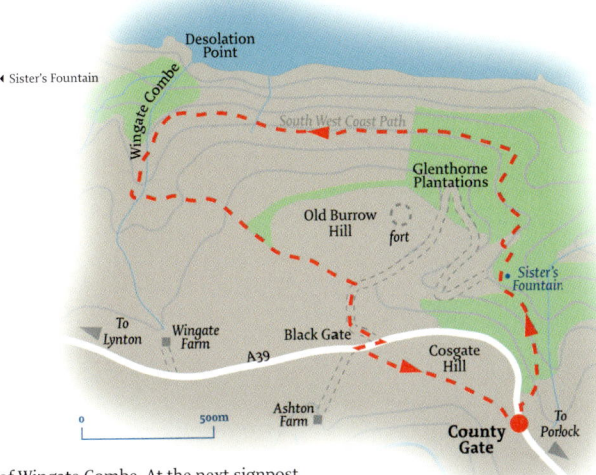

of Wingate Combe. At the next signpost, follow the sign for the Coast Path to Lynmouth, between stone pillars and past a house as the road bends left.

The track winds around the hillside. At the next sign, turn left off the track to continue on the Coast Path. This narrow path climbs gently and you'll stay on it for some time, passing some moss-covered stone seats and rhododendron bushes.

Eventually, the path turns left into Wingate Combe with a stream below. At a signpost, as the path turns back on itself, take the permitted footpath signed for County Gate via Old Burrow. The tiny path, not the easiest for the less mobile, makes its way up through trees, crossing a stream twice as it climbs steeply.

After around 10 minutes, you come to a gate. Go through this and continue to climb to a sign. Carry on up into the field, keeping close to the fence on the right.

At a stile, go over and walk alongside a stand of trees on the right to a metal gate. Head up over the field, following the sign on your right for County Gate. In the centre of the field is the Old Burrow Roman fortlet. Constructed in the mid-first century AD, it comprised an inner fortlet defended by two ditches and a rampart, and a further outer rampart with a single ditch.

Reaching the other side of the field, look for a five-bar wooden gate. You're still heading for County Gate. Once through, keep to the left-hand boundary and over to a road. Cross to a lay-by and look for a signpost for County Gate. Follow the grass track back to the car park.

South of Exford

Distance 7.5km **Time** 2 hours 30
Terrain steady climb up to Room Hill and steep descent into Curr Cleave
Map OS Explorer OL9 **Access** Exmoor National Park car park in Exford

This walk climbs above Exford and crosses fields and moorland before a steep drop takes you into a quiet valley as you follow the River Exe. The headwaters of the Exe are a haven for aquatic invertebrates and birds, and much work is being done in the region to restore and maintain this important peatland habitat.

From the car park entrance, turn left onto the main road. Go over the bridge by the 16th-century Exmoor White Horse Inn and turn left.

Walk up the road. As the road bends sharp right, go left down the access road to Court Farm, passing a public bridleway signpost for Room Hill (this may, at various times, be obscured by foliage).

Entering Court Farm, you'll spot a signpost – head for Room Hill. The route turns right at Court House. Go through a gate and onto a stony track.

Eventually, the route leaves the trees behind, just as you enter a field. Keep on the track across the field. As you enter the next field, turn right, again following a sign for Room Hill. The route runs close to the right-hand boundary and enters another field. Carry on ahead, through two more gates.

Where the grassy path splits, you can go either way as they join up a few metres later. At a signpost, turn left for Nethercote, crossing open land. Reaching the next signpost, at a path junction, turn left onto the bridleway for Winsford. The

path cuts through grass and ferns, with another track later joining from the right. Continue to make your way downhill.

At a post carrying the blue bridleway marking, the path becomes narrow and stony as it winds its way down into the valley and meets the River Exe. Once at the valley bottom, cross a footbridge. At the next sign, head uphill for Lyncombe.

Turn left at the next sign, again for Lyncombe. The Exe is now on your left as you walk through this steep-sided valley. After passing the scattering of buildings that make up Lyncombe, largely a 16th- or 17th-century farmhouse and outbuildings, a sign on the left offers two options back to Exford.

Choose the footpath which cuts across a field. Ignore the alternative footpath at a gate, which involves crossing the Exe, and look for a stile in the corner of the field. Go over this and through kissing gates.

The path now runs close to a boundary and the river on the left, crossing fields and open grassland before climbing up over a field to a stile alongside a gate. Go over the stile and down the track signed for Exford.

Approaching Court Farm, go through a gate and turn right. Follow the path to return to the car park.

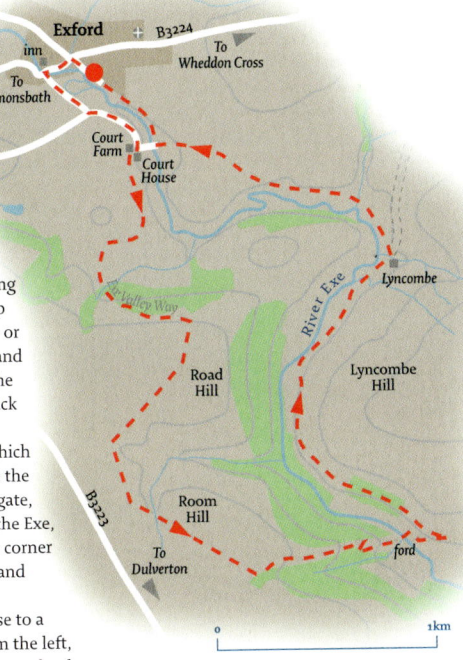

◀ Steep-sided valley close to Lyncombe

Exford to Prescott

Distance 3.25km **Time** 1 hour
Terrain easy walking with a few climbs, most notably from the car park to church
Map OS Explorer OL9 **Access** Exmoor National Park car park in Exford

This easy stroll around the northern reaches of Exford, an archetypal picturesque Exmoor village, passes through deserted medieval farmsteads and lush countryside. Exford hosts the long-established Exford Show every August when the region's finest local horses, ponies and sheep are spruced up and paraded.

From the car park entrance, turn right and walk up Church Hill to reach the 15th-century church where you'll spot a footpath sign on the left. Go through two gates and follow a track alongside a field. At a split, keep right and clamber over a stile beside a gate; you'll notice a yellow waymark here.

The track drops and bends left, with a stream joining briefly on the right. After traversing it via a footbridge, go through a gate, turning right for Prescott. The path, flanked by high-sided banks, runs along a field boundary to another gate. Don't go through this: instead, bear left up a track running adjacent to a fence to reach a five-bar gate, left of a stone dwelling.

Go through and continue towards Prescott. Cross a stream, go through a gate and climb a field to a large tree. Go through a gate left of the tree and head across the middle of the next field.

Passing a stand of trees, find a wooden gate on the edge of a small wood. Go through and keep left against the tree border. After around 30m, bend left, following the footpath sign down to a gate. You've now reached the dilapidated stone buildings that once made up Prescott – formerly the site of two farms.

Ignore the path bending left on approaching the first building. Continue up a slight incline, between the old dwellings. At the next sign, bear left. Walk for a short distance to another sign, turning right up over the field to a gate. Go through this and follow the sign for Exford via Coombe Farm to walk straight ahead.

After heading down over the field, go through a wooden gate and over a stepped stile, then turn right, keeping snug to another tree-lined boundary.

Reaching a fence, turn left and walk down the field towards the sound of running water, the source hidden by trees. At a signpost, head towards a telegraph pole and footbridge.

Cross the bridge and turn left. At the next five-bar gate, keeping the stream on your left, go through and on towards a stone building.

Don't go through the next five-bar gate. Instead, keep right in the direction of Exford. Follow the boundary to another gate, passing Coombe Farm and a stone dwelling on your left. Carry on up to a metal gate and join a track, turning left to head towards Exford.

The tarmac track leads down to Exford. Meeting a T-junction, with a children's play area ahead, turn left onto Park Street and at the junction cross to the car park.

◀ On the way to Prescott

Dunkery Beacon

Distance 3.5km **Time** 1 hour
Terrain easy walking **Map** OS Explorer OL9
Access parking at Dunkery Gate, around 3km northwest of Wheddon Cross

This short walk to the highest point on Exmoor and in Somerset offers sweeping views in every direction. It has been visited by humans since the Bronze Age, and exploring Dunkery and the beacon are a must for any holiday itinerary. The heather-covered hill is part of a Site of Special Scientific Interest and National Nature Reserve, and is managed by the National Trust.

From the car park, cross the road and join the path starting at the NT Dunkery stone pillar. The route is signed across the road for Exford, although you won't end up there.

The stony path climbs gradually and is bordered by heather, as is much of this route. Pick the right time of year and you'll be treated to a feast of colour. In summertime, the hill looks resplendent in its cloak of purple, but any month is special, even a blustery winter's day.

Bear in mind, however, that this is a popular area and something of a honeypot site during the holiday seasons.

An early morning start is recommended.

The route heads in a northwesterly direction. After nearly 2km, you meet a path crossing your route. Turn right and keep on this path to the beacon. The stone beacon at the summit of Exmoor was erected in September 1935 to commemorate the handing over of Dunkery Hill to the National Trust for the benefit of the nation by Sir Thomas Acland, Colonel Wiggin and Allan Hughes.

In days gone by, Dunkery Beacon was used as a fire signal station. Since prehistoric times, hilltops like this were used not only for keeping watch for potential invaders but passing on warnings by setting beacons alight.

In June 1977, the Silver Jubilee of Queen Elizabeth II, throngs of people made their way to see the beacon set alight, just one of many across the UK.

At the beacon, several routes lead off in different directions. Locate the stone pillar, which was presented by the AA and shows you're 1705 feet above sea level, and pick the path to its right which heads off in an SSE direction towards the car park. This leads you down off the hill in just under 1km to meet the road. Turn right and return to the car park.

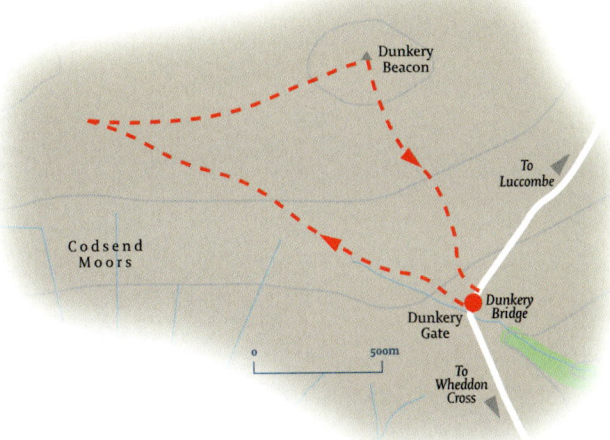

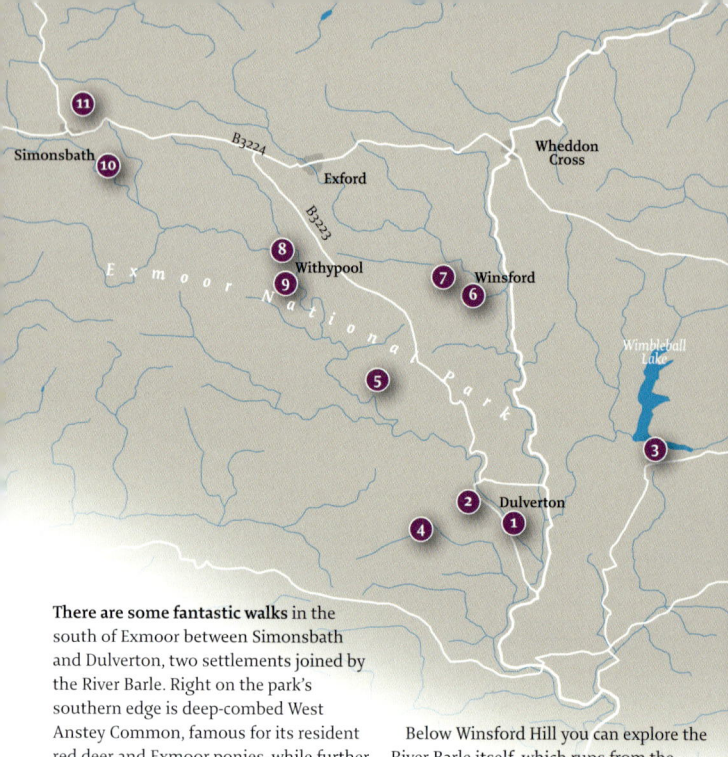

There are some fantastic walks in the south of Exmoor between Simonsbath and Dulverton, two settlements joined by the River Barle. Right on the park's southern edge is deep-combed West Anstey Common, famous for its resident red deer and Exmoor ponies, while further north, around Winsford, you're spoilt for choice. Winsford Hill is a wonderful heath-covered common where wild Exmoor ponies also happily roam and where you'll find The Punchbowl, a unique geological feature which, according to legend, is the result of the devil scooping out a well. After removing the soil, he threw it over his shoulder and formed Dunkery Hill in the process. Of course, a more logical explanation is that it was created during the ice age.

Below Winsford Hill you can explore the River Barle itself, which runs from the high plateau of The Chains above Simonsbath to Exebridge, where it joins the River Exe. Drop down into a wooded valley and visitors are treated to Tarr Steps, an ancient clapper bridge which spans the Barle. A honeypot site during the tourist season, it's among the national park's most photographed sites.

Further east, Wimbleball Lake (actually a man-made reservoir) is a beautiful spot popular with birdwatchers, sailors and paddleboarders, as well as walkers.

River Barle and South Exmoor

1 Dulverton and Brushford circular 34
Leave town and follow the Barle before returning through farmland

2 West of Dulverton 36
Cross the five-arch Barle Bridge for a circular country walk

3 Wimbleball Lake and Haddon Hill 38
The view over this beautiful reservoir – a popular spot for watersports – is well worth the effort

4 West Anstey Common 40
Explore one of Exmoor's most remote unenclosed landscapes

5 Winsford Hill to Tarr Steps 42
Take the high road to reach a rare medieval clapper bridge

6 The Punchbowl and The Allotment 44
Start high and make your way around to a charming village often called the prettiest on Exmoor

7 Winsford to Bye Common 46
Strike out from a picturesque village into the surrounding countryside before following the River Exe back

8 Withypool to Landacre Bridge 48
Go from bridge to bridge on this easy tour that follows the River Barle

9 Withypool Hill 50
As well as great summit views, there's the chance to look out for a less known ancient stone circle

10 Simonsbath and the Barle Valley 52
Meander through some wonderful scenery, looking out for an Iron Age fort and old industry along the way

11 Simonsbath and Prayway Head 54
Follow part of the coast-to-coast Two Moors Way through empty valleys before detouring to see the source of the Exe

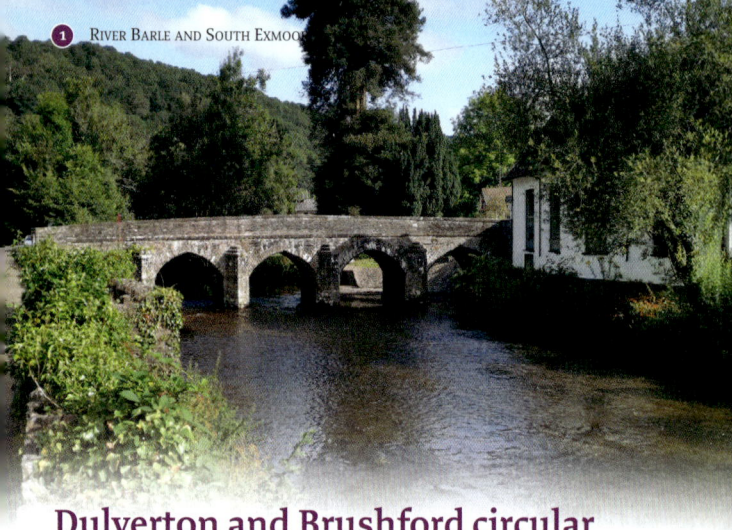

Dulverton and Brushford circular

Distance 8km **Time** 2 hours 30
Terrain occasional ascent, particularly climbing through woods towards Ashill Farm, and descent on return leg
Map OS Explorer 114 **Access** on-street parking or car parks in Dulverton

This circular walk south of the historic market town of Dulverton begins on the Exe Valley Way – a long-distance route which follows the length of the river valley for around 80km – before passing through the village of Brushford and across countryside and fields back to the starting point.

From the High Street, heading towards the bridge and the Bridge Inn, turn left into Chapel Street (signposted as a no-through road) which eventually becomes Millham Lane. Where the tarmac section ends, carry straight on to the end of the track.

Go through the kissing gate and cross the field, keeping the River Barle – which joins the Exe at Exebridge – close on the right. After crossing a few fields, you'll see footpath signs for Brushford.

On reaching a road, turn right. The road crosses the Barle and meets the B3222. Cross to Brushford New Road, alongside the garage, where you'll notice a footpath sign for the Circular Walk.

Continue through Brushford for about 500m, passing the parish hall and a crossroads. It's worth making a detour to the Church of St Nicholas – the highlight is the oldest parish chest in the country. Hollowed from an oak log, the chest was used to store parish registers and accounts, and for collecting alms.

Dulverton and Brushford circular

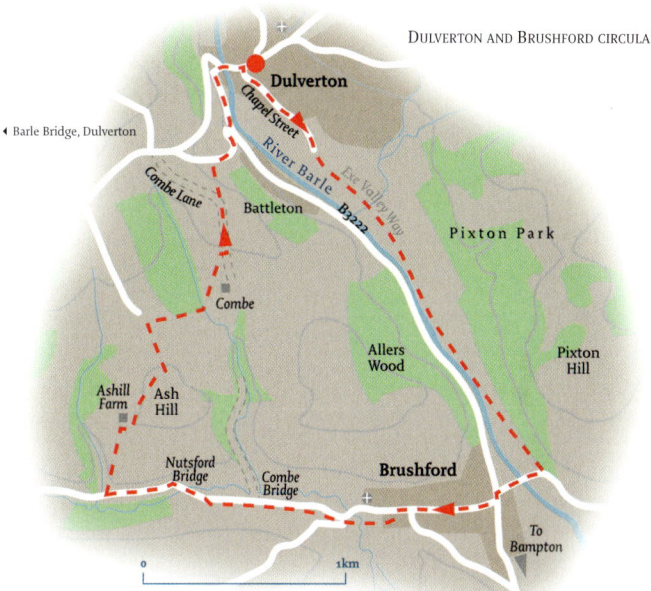

◀ Barle Bridge, Dulverton

Look for a sign on the left indicating the circular walk back to Dulverton. Take this route along the narrow path and through the metal kissing gate at the end, up steps and immediately right, following the Circular Walk sign.

You now head west for around 1km before turning right and going through a gate to a road. Turn left and follow this as it drops and bends. Look for a stile on your right and cross this into a field with a Circular Walk sign for Dulverton.

The path climbs through trees and out onto a field as you walk around Ashill Farm. Follow the yellow waymarkers over several fields, always keeping close to the left-hand boundary.

Eventually, you reach a gate to a stony track. Don't go through this. Instead, turn right at the gate and follow the footpath waymark, with the boundary on your left, down over fields and onto a muddy track leading around Combe Farm.

Your route takes you around some cottages on the right and up over a field to a tarmac drive. As the drive bends left at the top of the hill, you'll see a Circular Walk sign. Go through the gate and head for the field's bottom left-hand corner.

At a stile, under a canopy of trees, go over and follow the path heading off right, down to a road. Turn right and follow it to the B3222. Turn left and cross immediately, picking up a path running alongside a play area and the river. Return to Dulverton.

2 RIVER BARLE AND SOUTH EXMOOR

West of Dulverton

Distance 5.5km **Time** 2 hours
Terrain a few climbs but not particularly challenging **Map** OS Explorer OL9
Access car parks and roadside parking in Dulverton

This quiet, peaceful walk begins in the beautiful town of Dulverton, crosses the Barle and heads in a westerly direction, leaving the town's interesting shops, restaurants and pubs behind to explore a largely agricultural landscape. Dulverton became an important wool-working and trading town in the Middle Ages and the fresh water of the Barle was used to wash fleeces.

Cross the five stone arches of Dulverton Bridge (also known as Barle Bridge) and turn into Oldberry Lane. Follow this lane in the direction of Burridge Wood.

Reaching a junction on a sharp left bend, turn right, passing a no-through road sign and footpath sign for Burridge Wood. At a split, bear right onto the restricted byway, indicated by the plum marking. At a further split, next to a cottage, bear left for Beech Tree Cross. Join a narrow path climbing up through the woods, zigzagging to a wooden gate.

Go through and emerge from the trees into a field. Keep close to the right-hand boundary, heading for Beech Tree Cross. Continue up over the field to a gate. Go through, cross a tarmac track (leading down to Old Berry Farm) and pass through the small wooden gate opposite. Stroll across the field. At the boundary, go into the next field.

Keep high, close to the left-hand boundary. Head across the field, following the waymark post before descending to the bottom right-hand corner, crossing a stile and reaching a road.

Turn right onto the road and walk some 55m to a gate on the left, just after a house. Enter and drop down over the

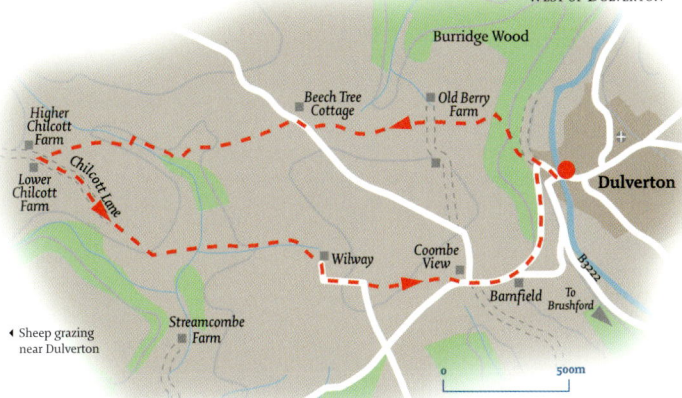

◀ Sheep grazing near Dulverton

field. Reaching the bottom, you'll see trees by a spring. The gate opposite carries the yellow-arrowed footpath plaque. Go through and turn left.

Walk along the lower section of this steep field, close to a stream. Look for a footbridge amongst the trees. Cross and turn right, following a grassy path close to the stream, now on your right. At the corner of the field, the route turns left and ascends, before passing through a gate into another field.

Once through, turn immediately right and go through a small gate. Cross the next field to a gate, hidden slightly by trees, in the far corner. Pass through and turn left onto unsigned Chilcott Lane.

Approaching a wooden gate in front of you, bear right in the direction indicated by the footpath plaque on the gatepost. The path runs between two fields. When you lose the trees on your right, carry on, close to the left-hand boundary, to a metal gate. Once through, drop down across the field to another gate. With water running past here, it can be muddy.

Climb up the next steep field, and go through a gate and onto a grassy path rising to a narrow tarmac track. Carry straight on past the entrance to Wilway (a house with outbuildings) and along the track. Just as it bends right, go through a gate marked with the footpath arrow on the rather hidden left-hand post.

Keep tight to the hedge on the left as you walk across the field. Go through into another field and down over the next to a further gate, after which you join a road with a bungalow on the left.

Follow the road, passing an Exmoor National Park sign on the left before a junction. Continue straight ahead for Dulverton. On reaching another turning on the left, opposite an entrance to a dwelling named Barnfield, bear left onto the road.

Walk down to the B3222, crossing Dulverton Bridge back to your car.

Wimbleball Lake and Haddon Hill

Distance 3.5km **Time** 1 hour
Terrain easy, but one climb to the top of Haddon Hill **Map** OS Explorer OL9
Access parking at Haddon Hill

This walk on the eastern fringes of Exmoor takes you around the southwestern tip of the spectacular Wimbleball Lake, a popular place for sailing managed by the South West Lakes Trust, before climbing to Haddon Hill and the Hadborough summit trig point for a great view of the lake.

At the entrance to the Haddon Hill car park, you'll see a sign for Wimbleball Dam. Go through the gate and walk down the tarmac road. Where the road splits, keep right.

At the fingerpost, head in the direction of Bury, down towards the water. Go through the gate alongside a cattle grid and you'll arrive at the dam. Walk across it to admire the ingenuity that went into constructing it in the late 1970s.

Although primarily acting as a reservoir, Wimbleball has become a popular destination for a host of activities, including fishing, sailing, cycling, walking or simply relaxing with a picnic. Exmoor National Park is a Dark Skies Reserve and there is a great designated camping area from which to enjoy the night sky.

Great care has been taken in the development of the lake with the planting of more than 12,000 trees native to Exmoor. This has attracted many forms

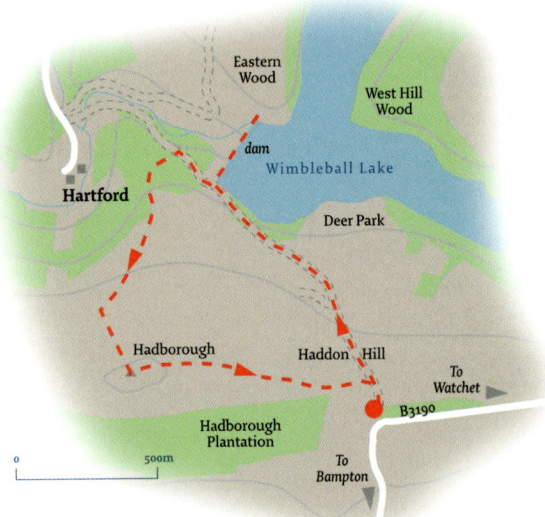

of wildlife and ornithologists are drawn to the area for its varied birdlife, including several members of the duck family, such as pochard, wigeon and teal.

Walk back across the 49m-high dam and turn right for Hartford. The tarmac track drops amongst trees and soon you'll spot a fingerpost. Take the footpath heading to the left for Haddon Hill. Climb the steps and go over a stile.

The track bends left and passes through a gate. Continue on the track until you meet a junction of paths, including a wide gravel track. Bear right and carry on up the stony track until you reach a yellow footpath sign. Turn left and follow the narrow path as it begins to climb up Haddon Hill, the largest area of heathland on the Brendon Hills.

There is always a good chance of seeing the free-roaming herd of Exmoor ponies that live around here. The oldest native pony breed in Britain, approximately 3500 of these ponies survive worldwide, of which around 350 live on Exmoor in around 20 different herds. None of them are wild, however, they all belong to someone, so it's essential to close all gates when walking on Exmoor.

There are several options and it's basically a case of making your own way to the Hadborough summit. You'll have fine views of the lake as you climb to finally reach the top, marked by a triangulation pillar. From this spot, there are several obvious paths returning to the car park.

◀ Dam at Wimbleball Lake

West Anstey Common

Distance 6.5km **Time** 2 hours
Terrain some ups and downs but nothing too strenuous, although you need to cross a ford **Map** OS Explorer OL9
Access off-road parking at Anstey Gate, around 10km northeast of Dulverton

This route runs close to the southern fringes of Exmoor National Park with much of the walking around and over West Anstey Common. Now Open Access Land, public bridleways and paths criss-cross a landscape where Exmoor ponies roam. This large swathe of unenclosed countryside typifies the beauty and remoteness of Exmoor's moorlands and is also home to red deer, brown hare, buzzards and kestrels.

From Anstey Gate, head southwest. Don't follow the bridleway sign for Molland. Instead, your route runs close to the fenced boundary with the path descending to a track and cattle grid.

On reaching the cattle grid, turn left and follow the track; it eventually turns into a narrow tarmac road. Reaching a turning on your right for Yeo Mill, take the bridleway on the left, just before the roadsign, marked Hawkridge.

This route heads up over Guphill Common and onto West Anstey Common, soon reaching Ridge Road. Cross and continue for Hawkridge. This area isn't waymarked and the route is indiscernible much of the way across grassy, tussocky land.

Head across this in a northeasterly direction to join a path which is part of the Two Moors Way, although not signed at this point. Then, drop down towards

trees, passing a boundary stone inscribed with Venford.

It's believed that this stone on Anstey Money Common dates from the 19th century and marks the boundary of nearby Venford Farm.

Eventually, the path reaches a road. Turn left, following it down and across the bridge over Dane's Brook, a tributary of the River Barle. The road now ascends, passing the entrance to Zeal Farm. Just past a barn, look for a public bridleway on the left for Anstey Gate.

Cross two fields to Zeal Farm. Go through the farm gate by the farmhouse and drop down to the blue-capped gatepost. The path descends back to Dane's Brook; there is no bridge, only stepping stones, and care is needed.

Once across the river, head uphill for Anstey Gate. Again, it's a path which isn't always clear but if you keep walking west and don't turn off on any intersecting paths you'll return to the start.

There are around 4000 red deer roaming Exmoor and, depending on the time of year, you may see some on the common here. Although for most of the time stags and hinds live apart, they come together in autumn for the rut, or mating season. At that time of year you are more likely to hear the impressive bellowing roar of the stag, known locally as 'bolving', echoing in the combes and over the moorland.

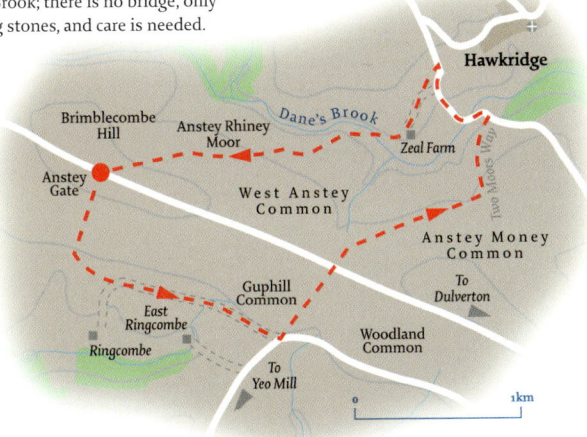

Winsford Hill to Tarr Steps

Distance 8.75km **Time** 2 hours 30
Terrain easy walk, although there is a steady climb up onto Varle Hill
Map OS Explorer OL9 **Access** lay-by at Spire Cross, where Halse Lane from Winsford meets the B3223

Beginning high up on Winsford Hill, this walk heads to the tiny settlement of Knaplock before reaching Tarr Steps at one of Exmoor's most visited spots. This ancient Grade I-listed clapper bridge is a splendid 17-span specimen regarded as the longest in the country.

At the crossroads, where the roadside fingerpost carries the name Spire Cross, head in the direction of Knaplock for about 500m. Where the road bends left over a cattle grid, follow the public bridleway for Tarr Steps. The route enters Knaplock Estate.

Follow the wide stony track which eventually becomes tarmac. On a bend, you'll notice a path joining on the right. Ignore this and continue to Knaplock.

The track descends into Higher Knaplock (passing Higher Knaplock Farm) and around to Knaplock. On reaching farm buildings, look for a signpost in the hedge on your right. You have a choice: take the footpath to Tarr Steps heading left or, as described here, continue on the bridleway, passing the few houses making up Knaplock.

This track is known as Watery Lane and drops into woodland with water running to your left. At a split, carry on for Tarr Steps. After a few metres, turn left and cross a footbridge. The River Barle is now on your right. Continue to Tarr Steps, around 800m away. Reaching a fingerpost, take the permitted footpath which drops closer to the river as it leads towards the clapper bridge.

Winsford Hill to Tarr Steps

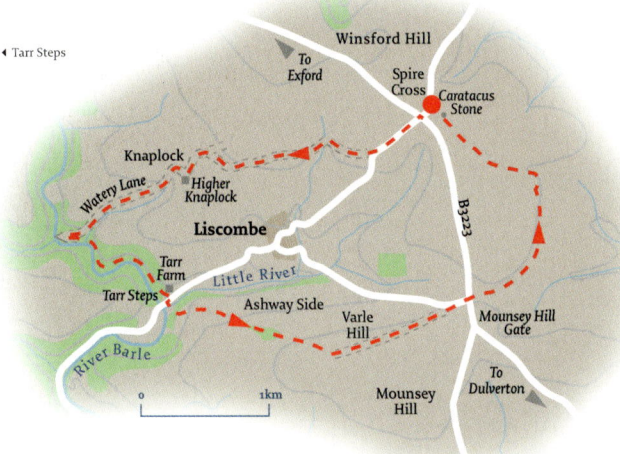

◀ Tarr Steps

This iconic clapper bridge is built without mortar or cement and could date back to the Bronze Age. Local legend has it that the steps must have been laid by the devil (they are very heavy), and apparently an unlucky black cat that once attempted the crossing disappeared in a puff of smoke!

Once you've explored the site, head for Ashway and Varle Hill, crossing the small footbridge. After a few metres, by a gate, the narrow path climbs up on the left.

Reaching another sign, head for Varle Hill by climbing up over Ashway Side. Emerge from the trees and continue on the grassy track, heading uphill, ignoring paths on both sides. This stretch of the walk is lacking in signs so you'll have to follow your nose to eventually reach a gate. Carry on for Winsford from here.

At a crossroads of paths, go straight on for Mounsey Hill. On meeting a road, cross a cattle grid and walk to the B3223. Cross this onto a bridleway, heading for Winsford.

The path leads down towards a gate in a field. Don't go through this – instead, follow the path as it bends left, keeping close to the field boundary. After a while, you'll see a sign against the bank. Head for Spire Cross.

As the track bends sharp right, a sign informs walkers to turn left for Spire Cross. Just before reaching Spire Cross, you'll see the Caratacus Stone, an inscribed marker post, possibly dating from the 6th century, protected by a shelter built in 1906. Caractacus was the British leader of a rebellion against the Roman occupation in 47-51AD.

The Punchbowl and The Allotment

Distance 7.5km **Time** 2 hours 30
Terrain there is a steady drop to Winsford and similar climb to the top of Winsford Hill on your return **Map** OS Explorer OL9
Access travelling away from Exford on the B3223, look for a small car park on the left with a post at the entrance signalling a public bridleway to Halse Lane

This pleasant walk starts high up on Exmoor, atop Winsford Hill, before skirting the distinctive landmark called The Punchbowl and descending to the attractive village of Winsford. This marks the halfway point before returning to the car park via The Allotment, an open stretch of grassland.

From the car park, head in the direction of the public bridleway marker post for Halse Lane. The path passes a little hollow on the right containing a solitary tree. A grassy track joins from the right; your route bends left before splitting three ways. Select the middle path, heading downhill towards fields. You're now at the head of The Punchbowl.

Given the shape of The Punchbowl, it has been suggested that this was the site of the only glacier on Exmoor during the Pleistocene ice ages. More fanciful is the theory that the devil himself scooped out the land here and threw it over his shoulder, thus creating Dunkery Hill.

Descend towards fields. On reaching a tree-lined boundary and gate, go through. Walk down the field, keeping the fence close on the right.

When you reach another fence at the bottom, go through the gate in the right-hand corner, turning immediately left for Withycombe. Walk down the track towards a farm.

The track crosses Winn Brook via a wooden planked bridge before entering Withycombe Farm. Passing barns, turn right and up the drive. At the top,

THE PUNCHBOWL AND THE ALLOTMENT

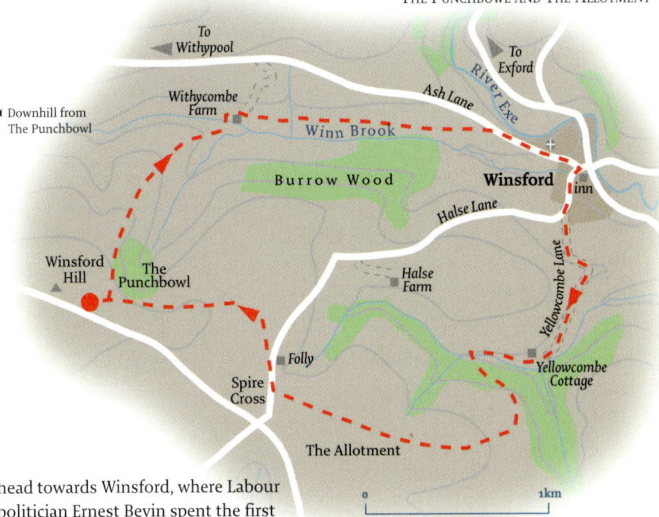

head towards Winsford, where Labour politician Ernest Bevin spent the first eight years of his life in the 1880s.

Soon, go through a gate and across six fields, keeping a boundary close on your right. After the sixth field, go through a gate and follow a narrow path running close to trees. Dwellings will appear on your left.

You'll eventually emerge onto a road, known as Ash Lane. Turn right and walk down to Winsford. Cross a ford via the footbridge and begin the return stage of the walk up Halse Lane with the thatched Royal Oak Inn, a 12th-century former farmhouse/dairy, on the left. Walk up the road, but just before it bends sharp right, take the track – Yellowcombe Lane – on the left. The path bends, climbs and passes through gates before reaching Yellowcombe Cottage.

Follow the footpath, which is not overly discernible in places, around the cottage and cross a stream before climbing up through the woods. At a junction of footpaths, turn sharp left for Summerway and Spire Cross.

The path climbs and leaves the trees behind upon reaching the edge of the area of grassland called The Allotment. At a signpost, turn right for Spire Cross. Carry on across The Allotment towards a building in the distance.

At the end, go through a gate and follow the track to the right towards a road. Opposite the building called Folly, join a grassy track. It splits twice – keep left both times and walk straight ahead upon reaching a crossroads of paths.

The path reaches the top of The Punchbowl and, soon after, the car park.

7 RIVER BARLE AND SOUTH EXMOOR

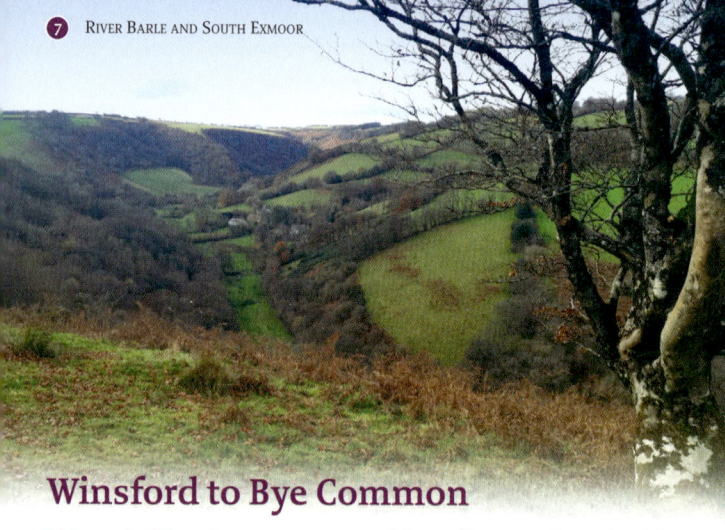

Winsford to Bye Common

Distance 9km **Time** 2 hours 30
Terrain some ups and downs
Map OS Explorer OL9 **Access** car park
at Winsford

From the pretty village of Winsford, with its thatched cottages, charming seasonal tea garden and 12th-century farmhouse which is now a cosy pub, this walk heads west onto Bye Common where there are views aplenty before returning alongside the River Exe. This area was the hunting ground of the gentleman highwayman Tom Faggus in the 17th century who was said to lie in wait for wealthy patrons of the local inn at closing time.

From the car park, with the garage on your left and tea garden on your right, turn right and head up Ash Lane. Pass the church and continue up the road until you pass the Winsford village sign. On the right, you'll see a metal gate signed for Exford and Larcombe Foot. Go through.

After around 100m, bear left uphill, signed for Exford via Bye Common. The path climbs up between trees and passes through three gates. As you go through the third, turn right and then immediately left. The path now runs close to a field boundary on your left with fine views down into the valley on the right.

When you reach a junction of paths, carry on for Nethercote. Go through another gate and on to a large five-bar gate by a signpost. Go through and follow the grassy track up towards the middle of the field before heading to a small gate in the bottom right-hand corner. Enter the next field, keeping the boundary close on your right.

Continue to another gate. Pass through and head towards a signpost at a gate in

◀ Bye Common

front of you. Go through the metal gate and turn immediately left, with the field boundary close to your left-hand side.

The path drops to the River Exe where you'll meet a track and signpost. Turn right onto the bridleway heading to Larcombe Foot. The dirt track runs close to the river for some distance until you reach a gate at a bridge, next to the Exford-Winsford road.

Before the bridge, turn right onto the footpath for Winsford. Go through a gate and keep the river on your left. Carry on until you reach a signpost which you'll recognise from your outward journey.

Continue for Winsford, reaching the metal gate and Ash Lane within a few metres. Turn left and walk down to Winsford. As well as the legendary Tom Faggus, Winsford is closely associated with some other famous names. Former Prime Minister Boris Johnson grew up on the family farm at Nethercote and, at the opposite end of the political spectrum, it was also the birthplace of Ernest Bevin, respected statesman, trade union leader and Foreign Secretary who played a crucial role in the creation of NATO.

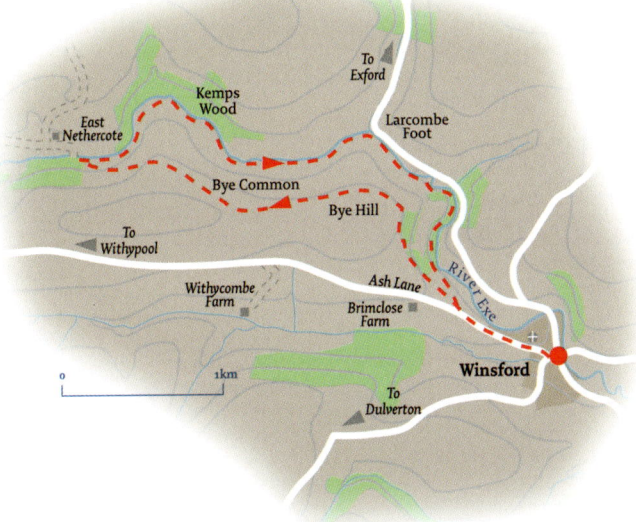

RIVER BARLE AND SOUTH EXMOOR

Withypool to Landacre Bridge

Distance 7.25km **Time** 2 hours
Terrain straightforward walk
Map OS Explorer OL9 **Access** car park in Withypool, close to the bridge

A walk between two distinctive bridges spanning the River Barle and overlooked by the open expanse of Withypool Common, this route begins in the village of Withypool with its red sandstone six-arch bridge. From here, it heads west to the medieval five-arch Landacre Bridge before returning via a riverbank stroll.

From the car park, cross the bridge and pass Withypool's post office and shop before taking the steps on the left which bring you to the road above the post office. Turn left and then right following the footpath sign for Kitridge Lane.

The path veers left of the Old School and cuts up through fields and a kissing gate to lead onto Kitridge Lane. Turn left, in the direction of Simonsbath, and follow the lane for around 1.5km as it climbs steadily. For a time, follow the Two Moors Way, the long-distance trail which covers 164km from Dartmoor to Exmoor.

At a gate, the tarmac lane is replaced by a stony track. Go through and onto the restricted byway, continuing until you meet a road. Turn left onto Landacre Lane and walk down to the distinctive Landacre Bridge. This Grade II-listed medieval multi-span bridge is a popular spot during clement weather.

To return to Withypool, walk up the road. Just past the lay-by, you'll see a sign for Withypool. The path, which isn't always the clearest, cuts across the landscape with the river down on the left

◂ Landacre Bridge

to reach a gate. Go straight through this for Withypool.

The route crosses open ground and several fields while following yellow waymarkers, always retaining a boundary close on the left.

At a signpost, upon approaching a house, you'll be directed up over a stile and across a footbridge before following the path around the outside of the field, over another stile and down past farm buildings at Brightworthy, around 1.5km from Withypool.

Soon, the Barle will be close to you again on the left and it's a case of following the river back to Withypool. The willow trees, or 'withies', that line the river give the village its name.

If looking for some refreshment following the walk, head past the post office again and carry on along the road to soon reach the Royal Oak Inn, an unassuming hostelry with some fascinating historical connections. R D Blackmore wrote part of *Lorna Doone* whilst a guest here, and in the 1930s the pub was owned by Maxwell Knight, an MI5 spymaster credited with destroying the British fascist movement. Knight is said to have been Ian Fleming's inspiration for 'M', James Bond's boss. General Dwight D Eisenhower, supreme allied commander in the Second World War and later 34th President of the United States, was also a guest here while supervising preparations at nearby Woolacombe for the D-Day Landings.

Withypool Hill

Distance 5.25km **Time** 1 hour 30
Terrain easy walk, although there is a steady climb initially from the car park
Map OS Explorer OL9
Access car park in Withypool

The tiny village of Withypool with its quaint lime-washed cottages, high up on Exmoor, seems a world away from the hustle and bustle of modern-day life. This walk takes you south of the village to explore Withypool Hill and visit an ancient stone circle just a short distance from the cairn, first discovered in 1898 by a local farmer whose horse stumbled over the site.

From the car park, turn right and walk up the road which climbs with houses on your right. After passing the village hall and entrance to South Hill Farm on your left, continue up the road until you reach the start of an unsigned path on your right, just before the road bends left.

Follow the path, which cuts low across the northern slopes of Withypool Hill, before heading in a southwesterly direction on reaching a road. Now, you need to follow a footpath marked as a restricted byway to Willingford Bridge.

Around 500m along this path, look out for a small unsigned path on the left. This detours up to Withypool Hill's summit. You'll find a small cairn atop the 398m hill which offers wonderful views across one of Exmoor's more remote corners. It's worth taking the time to look for Withypool Stone Circle just below the hilltop.

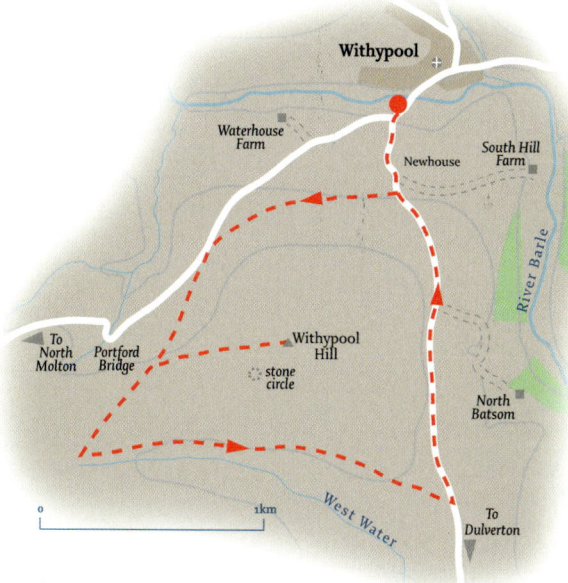

Around 30 small gritstones remain of the circle, although there may originally have been around 100. Most are now difficult to spot as surrounding vegetation has covered them up and there are conspicuous gaps on the northern and western side where stones have been removed, perhaps to be used in local road construction.

Although these parts of the national park have been inhabited since the Bronze Age, this is one of only two known circles on Exmoor; the other is Porlock Stone Circle. The areas with the most stone circles in Britain are those with the most available stone, such as Aberdeenshire and Dartmoor.

◀ On Withypool Hill

Return to the restricted byway and after about 500m, just as you approach a tree-lined boundary, you'll see a wide path on your left. It's unmarked and not the most defined, but it heads off across the lower slopes on the hill's southern side.

You're walking eastwards and will continue until you meet a road and cattle grid. Here, you have two choices: either turn left and walk down the road back to Withypool or keep left of the road on the grassy bank to make your way down towards the village. This keeps you off the road for the majority of the time.

10 RIVER BARLE AND SOUTH EXMOOR

Simonsbath and the Barle Valley

Distance 10km **Time** 3 hours
Terrain a few climbs and descents but not a particularly challenging walk
Map OS Explorer OL9 **Access** Ashcombe car park, close to the Exmoor Forest Inn

Starting in the 19th-century village of Simonsbath at the heart of Exmoor, this walk follows the River Barle southeast, passing the location of an Iron Age fort before returning via fields high above the Barle Valley.

Turn right out of Ashcombe car park and join the signed Picked Stones route opposite the Exmoor Forest Inn.

The narrow path winds up amongst trees before dropping to a sign. Head for Cow Castle, following part of the long-distance Two Moors Way for just under 5km. The River Barle is on your right all the way along the outward leg of this walk. You'll only lose sight of it momentarily as you walk around Flexbarrow and Cow Castle.

Just after passing Flexbarrow, look out for the ruins of a cottage and the long-forgotten, and unsuccessful, Wheal Eliza copper mine nearby. In 1858 this spot became notorious as the site of a shocking murder when the body of a labourer's daughter was found at the bottom of the flooded mineshaft. Her widower father was found guilty of the awful act, admitting that he preferred to spend what little money he had on drink than on care for his daughter – he was hanged in Taunton.

Continue following blue bridleway markings all the way to Cow Castle, an isolated hilltop with a commanding view over the River Barle. This was once an Iron Age hillfort and the 2m-high rampart and defensive ditch are easily seen.

Keep with the path as it weaves around

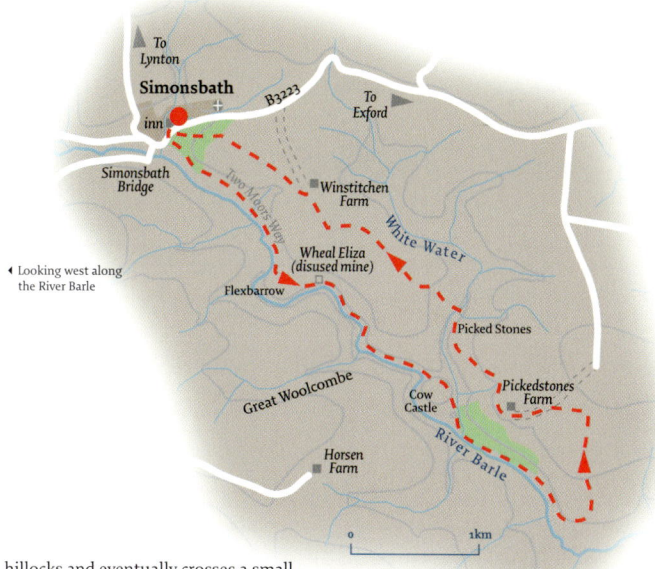

◀ Looking west along the River Barle

hillocks and eventually crosses a small footbridge next to a five-bar gate. Go straight on, ignoring another footbridge on your right, until you spot a sign for Picked Stones at a gate. Go through this and turn immediately left.

The less-defined route climbs steeply alongside the field boundary to a crossroads of paths. Turn left and cross the field, following the sign for Simonsbath via Picked Stones. You're now on the return leg of the walk.

Turn down the tarmac track to reach Pickedstones Farm and follow the bridleway for Simonsbath, which keeps high and offers occasional glimpses of the Barle down in the valley to your left.

After some time, the path drops steeply into a combe. Go over the small bridge crossing White Water and follow the path as it climbs steadily from the combe. At the end of the path, bend left and head for a stand of trees and a signpost.

Carry on, following the hedgerows, to reach the drive at Winstitchen Farm. Just before the farm itself, go left to pass through several fields before arriving at Birchcleave Wood. There are lots of paths in the woodland; keep straight ahead to make your way down to the village. When you reach the road, turn right to return to the car park.

Simonsbath and Prayway Head

Distance 6.8km **Time** 2 hours
Terrain some steep gradients but generally a straightforward walk
Map OS Explorer OL9 **Access** Ashcombe car park, close to the Exmoor Forest Inn

In bygone days, the area around the tiny village of Simonsbath was rife with banditry and smuggling. In the 1800s, smugglers exploited the area's wild, remote landscapes to move contraband from the north coast to be distributed across Somerset and Devon. The 350-year-old Simonsbath House, built by the first Warden of the Forest of Exmoor and now a welcoming hotel, was the focus for many of the smuggling tales of the era.

This walk begins in Simonsbath. From the higher level of Ashcombe car park, pick up the path for Prayway Head. This part of the walk is on the Two Moors Way.

The path climbs through Ashcombe Plantation. At the edge of the area of trees, the path turns left and drops to cross a stream. You'll be following yellow waymarkers here.

A few metres past the stream, look out for a gate and go through this, continuing for Prayway Head. The waymarked route climbs up over a field and across a small footbridge before sweeping around over another bridge.

The next stretch can get a little boggy as you head up to a metal gate. Go through this, turning left for Prayway Head. Enjoy the lovely views, especially on the left across to the moors.

Sitting at 325m above sea level, Simonsbath is situated in the heart of what was Exmoor's Royal Forest. In 1818, the Crown decided to sell the forest and it was acquired by the visionary industrialist John Knight in 1820 in what became the greatest land reclamation

Simonsbath and Prayway Head

◀ Ashcombe Bottom

England had ever seen. His plans involved attempting to create a grand estate out of the wild countryside. As well as introducing sheep to Exmoor, Knight created two farmsteads and built roads, walls and two canals. His plan for great iron ore mining projects to fund more development weren't as successful, however, and money shortages contributed to the venture never reaching its full potential.

On reaching the B3223, turn right and walk for around 250m to a lay-by on the left. Continue on the Two Moors Way, following the Exe Head sign, by bearing right through the gate and continuing to another gate. Once through this, follow the bridleway sign directing you left. Keep close to the fenced boundary.

At the next sign, you'll be turning left. However, at this point you can detour to Exe Head by crossing Dure Down to see where the River Exe begins its 96km journey to the English Channel.

The onward route heads down over fields on a bridleway, marked for Simonsbath. Pass sheep pens on reaching a gate and enter the next field.

Continue following the bridleway signs as the route runs along steep-sided Lime Combe, with Limecombe Cottage on your left in a secluded valley. Now a holiday cottage, it was originally two buildings and supposedly built for railway workers hired to work on a proposed line from Simonsbath to Porlock. Unfortunately, the venture never materialised.

You'll pass through a run of attractive trees before eventually reaching a moss-covered bridge. Follow the footpath to Simonsbath. This arrives at the B3358. Cross this road to pick up the Simonsbath footpath. After a few metres go through a gate and turn sharp left, following the signpost for Simonsbath Sawmill.

Follow the waymarked route with a leat and the River Barle on your right until you finally meet a road, by the sawmills. Turn left. At the road junction, turn right and return to the car park.

In the east of Exmoor are the Brendon Hills which, unlike the neighbouring upland areas of Exmoor and the Quantock Hills, are mainly cultivated farmland. With gentle valleys and working farms, the air of tranquillity which seems to exude from this part of the national park is a far cry from what life was like in the 19th century.

Back then, a shortlived mining enterprise was in full flow. The West Somerset Mineral Line snaked its way for around 19km from the Brendon Hills to the port of Watchet, where iron ore was transported to South Wales. By 1917, the line was gone, but much of the route can still be walked.

Many of the walks featured in this section are focused in and around the popular coastal town of Minehead, the start point for the South West Coast Path which ends 1014km away in Poole Harbour, Dorset. Medieval Dunster with its castle, yarn market and quaint streets is not far inland from Minehead and also makes a good base for exploring this quieter corner of the national park.

Minehead and the Brendon Hills

1 Roadwater to Treborough   58
Set out along the Coleridge Way on a circular walk around quiet woodlands and villages

2 Nettlecombe from Roadwater   60
With lovely views of the Brendon Hills, this rewarding circular walk also follows the Coleridge Way

3 North Hill   62
Enjoy fantastic sea views on this rugged rollercoaster walk from Minehead to Bossington Hill

4 Dunster and Conygar Tower   64
This short walk to a Victorian folly is a good introduction to a village packed with history and charm

5 Grabbist Hill and Dunster   66
Be thankful and inspired by all things bright and beautiful on this grand tour of heather-covered hills

6 Bossington Hill and Selworthy   68
Explore steep-sided combes and two charming villages on this walk above Hurlstone Point

7 Woodcombe and North Hill   70
Views over rolling pastureland and the rugged coast await on this short walk on the south side of the hill

8 Dunster and Bat's Castle   72
Stroll through woods, pastureland and heath on this climb to a well-preserved hillfort

Roadwater to Treborough

Distance 12km **Time** 3 hours
Terrain a straightforward walk with one climb up through woods after Comberow
Map OS Explorer OL9 **Access** considerate roadside parking in Roadwater where it can be narrow in places

Exploring a quiet corner of the Brendon Hills, this walk follows part of the Coleridge Way – an 82km long-distance route established in 2005 linking several sites associated with the Romantic poet Samuel Taylor Coleridge, including Nether Stowey, his former home.

From Roadwater's village hall, walk past the shop and along the road, passing Watersmeet Close. Take the immediate left by the Old Bridge Post Office, which is Harper's Lane, although unsigned.

Pass a no-through road on the right, signed for the Old Mineral Line, continuing up the hill. Opposite a cottage, turn right onto a bridleway for Sticklepath. Follow it along the bottom of a steep field and into Erridge Wood.

Eventually, the bridleway bends left and drops to a field. Go through the gate, across the little bridge and up through the next gate. After a short distance, the path forks. Keep left. At a crossroads of paths, continue straight ahead for Sticklepath.

Reaching Pit Wood, you arrive at a wide area where the track branches in several directions. Pick the route dropping to the right which zigzags down to the drive for Pitt Mill. At the bottom, turn left and walk up the track (a nearby signpost is marked for Comberow). Keep straight ahead through woodland, ignoring a footpath sign you'll see on your left soon after a stone house.

At a path junction, keep straight ahead on the path marked for Leigh Barton before ignoring the next Leigh Barton sign on your right. Continue until you see the cottages of Comberow. Here, you can detour and climb steps by a tunnel to see The Incline, the steepest section of what

ROADWATER TO TREBOROUGH

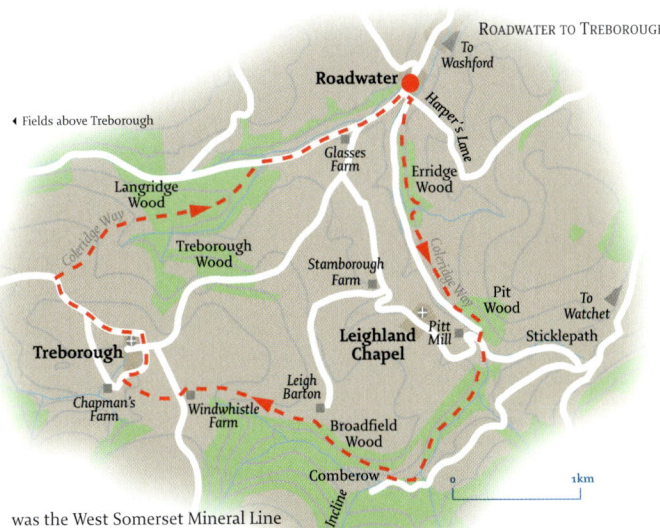

◂ Fields above Treborough

was the West Somerset Mineral Line Railway. Built in the mid-19th century, the line was used to carry iron ore from the Brendon Hills to the harbour at Watchet. Rising 245m over a distance of 1.2km, the Incline was a fantastic piece of Victorian engineering ingenuity in its day.

Return to the cottages and follow the footpath for Brendon Hill via Leigh Barton. Go over the bridge and bear right onto the path for Leighland Chapel. The path zigzags up through the woods.

At a signpost, turn left onto a permitted footpath, bearing right for Treborough at the next sign to climb up through Broadfield Wood. Reaching a farmyard, head towards Coldharbour. Walk up the track and go through a gate into a field. The route runs along the valley, keeping high with the field boundary on your right. Go through the next gate and follow the narrow sunken lane to a signpost. Bear left, pass Windwhistle Farm and emerge onto a road.

Cross this and go through a gate in the direction of Treborough. Walk down the field, keeping straight ahead to a gate. Turn right onto the road and walk up to the tiny village of Treborough.

At the crossroads, keep straight ahead, passing the church on your left. Follow the narrow road for some time until you reach a signpost on your right. Here, take the footpath through the gate on your right for Roadwater. Head down over two fields until you reach a kissing gate in the corner of the field.

Go through this and head across to two gates. Take the track through Langridge Wood. Continue ahead at the signpost with the feather, indicating the Coleridge Way. The track drops down to a road. Turn right and walk back to Roadwater.

Nettlecombe from Roadwater

Distance 9km **Time** 2 hours 30
Terrain an easy walk, although there is a steep field to climb **Map** OS Explorer OL9
Access roadside parking in Roadwater

Tucked away in a deep wooded valley, Roadwater is best known for its associations with the long-gone West Somerset Mineral Line. This walk takes in a stretch of the 82km-long Coleridge Way, named after the Romantic poet, with woods, pastures and views of the Brendon Hills among the delights.

From Roadwater's village hall, walk past the shop and along the road, passing Watersmeet Close. Take the immediate left by the Old Bridge Post Office, which is Harper's Lane, although unsigned.

Pass a no-through road on the right, signed for the Old Mineral Line, continuing up the hill. Around a bend, turn right off the lane, marked as a bridleway to Sticklepath. Pass through a gate, following the grass track along the bottom of a steep field. Beyond the next gate, you enter Erridge Wood.

After around 500m, the path splits. Keep left, heading to a small gate. Go through this, across a field, over a spring and then turn right to the next gate.

Beyond another wooden gate, you'll leave the trees behind and continue along part of the Coleridge Way. At a crossroads of paths, continue ahead for Sticklepath. Pass through two more gates, heading for Sticklepath. At the next signpost, carry on into Pit Wood. Arriving at a junction of wide paths, choose the ascending route, which is identified by a blue bridleway mark on a tree.

When you reach the end of a field, go through a gate and carry straight on along the permitted footpath to Chidgley. After skirting farm buildings, turn right at the road, then immediately left by the Royal Mail letterbox.

Follow the footpath for Nettlecombe through what looks like a garden entrance and onto a grassy track running along the foot of a steep field. Eventually, at a gate, the footpath heads towards the bottom right-hand corner of a field. Go over two

NETTLECOMBE FROM ROADWATER

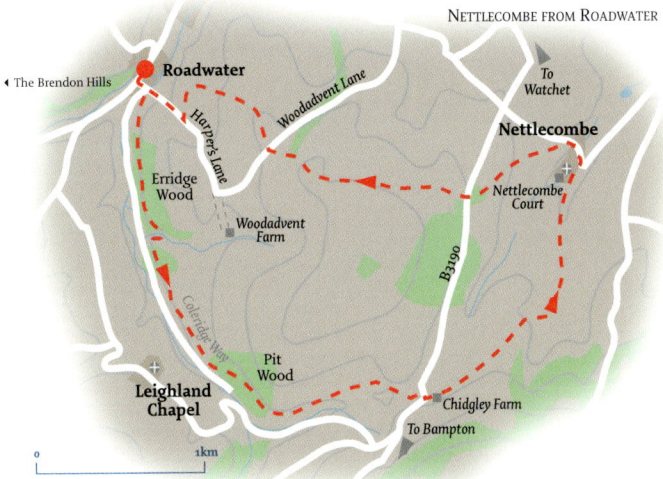

stiles and continue on the path clinging to the left-hand boundary.

In time, this brings you to a gate. Go through and pass a stone barn and house. Just before the track bends right, keep left for Nettlecombe. Edging a field, the footpath reaches Nettlecombe Court, a magnificent property once held by Prince Godwine, son of King Harold. Set in a secluded wooded valley, it's a fine blend of medieval, Elizabethan, Tudor and Georgian architecture. Following the Battle of Hastings, William the Conqueror got the keys and it was passed down through the Trevelyan baronets until the early 20th century. It is now the Leonard Wills Field Centre run by the Field Studies Council, an educational charity, since 1967.

Head straight on through the entrance flanked by two pillars with horse busts. Turn left onto a tarmac lane, passing the church and climbing to a split. Carry straight on, through a gate, following the bridleway sign.

Shortly after the gate, turn left (ignoring the car park entrance) to take a grassy track in the direction of Roadwater to a gate. Head up over a steep field, keeping close to the left-hand boundary to find a gate in the extreme left-hand corner. Go over the stile and up through the woods, following yellow waymarkers on the trees to a gate opening onto a road.

Cross the road and continue for Roadwater, just under 2.5km away, going over fields and stiles whilst always heading for the village.

Eventually, the footpath drops and meets Woodadvent Lane. A sign opposite directs you through another field. Follow the footpath for some time, going through various ungated entrances and more stiles before reaching Harper's Lane. Turn right and return to Roadwater.

North Hill

Distance 12km **Time** 3 hours
Terrain some steep ascents/descents on the Rugged Coast Path on the outward leg **Map** OS Explorer OL9 **Access** look for a concrete lay-by on the right on the climb up Hill Road from Minehead, just before the road levels off after a campsite

One of the best in the region, this ridge walk stretches from Minehead to Bossington and takes in the glorious North Hill. From the summit, the Bristol Channel and the Welsh Coast is on one side and the unfolding Exmoor landscape on the other.

As long ago as the 1800s, North Hill was the site of a large military training base. It was under military control again during the Second World War, with a radar station and tank marshalling area. Exmoor played a vital role in the training of allied troops for D-Day and the concrete bases of Nissen huts are still visible.

Near the entrance to the lay-by, follow a grassy path, flanked by three pine trees, heading in the opposite direction to the woods. Where the wide path splits, keep right, enjoying excellent views of the Bristol Channel.

At a bench and fingerpost, go straight on for the signed Coast Path to Bossington, turning right at the next sign for the Rugged Coast Path. The path drops and splits after a bench on your right. Bear left and head to a gate. Go through and begin the Rugged Coast Path in earnest as it descends steeply. You'll stay on the same path along the length of North Hill.

This dramatic walk weaves in and out of

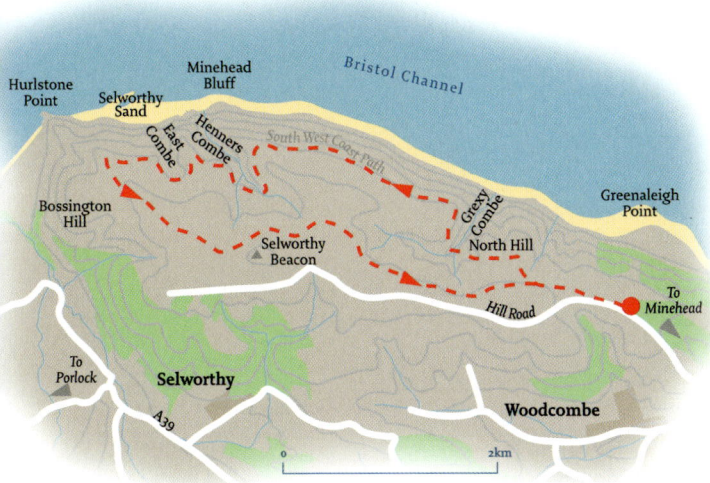

three deep combes – Grexy, Henners and East – the path clinging to the edge with precipitous drops in places. While Grexy's eastern arm was the location for a medieval farmstead, now only visible as earthworks, two post-medieval quarry pits lie on the spur between Henners and East Combe.

Climbing out of East Combe, you'll see a sign. Don't turn left; continue along the Rugged Coast Path. Further on, keep left where the path splits. Eventually, it bends to the left. Here, admire fine views of Porlock Bay and beyond.

At the next signed junction, where a path joins on the right, carry on up, following the sign for the Coast Path to Minehead. Carry straight on at the next junction and head in the direction of the acorn emblem, bearing left at the following one.

Continue back along the hill, always following the acorn sign in the direction of Minehead. Eventually, you'll be back on familiar ground, passing a junction of paths and the bench seen on the outward leg of the walk as you return to the lay-by.

◀ Beginning the Rugged Coast Path

Dunster and Conygar Tower

Distance 2.5km **Time** 1 hour
Terrain easy but with a steep climb
Map OS Explorer OL9 **Access** buses to Dunster Steep from Taunton, and Exmoor Coaster bus from Watchet, Minehead, Porlock and Lynmouth; car park at Dunster Steep

Many sights are packed into this short walk around the medieval village of Dunster, including an historic yarn market and splendid castle overlooking the main street. Originally constructed in timber during the 11th century, it's been remodelled over the years and boasts fine gardens. Then there's Conygar Tower, a red sandstone folly built in 1775.

From the car park, turn right and walk down Dunster Steep. Just before the traffic lights, cross the road and head towards Minehead. Don't enter the subway but continue along the path, passing a bus stop.

Ignore the permitted footpath to Dunster signpost and walk alongside the road. You'll see two posts marking what was the old Minehead to Dunster road. Continue until you reach a wide footpath on your left marked for Dunster. Take this path, heading upwards. Ignore the first right turn but take the next. If you reach an old quarry on your right, you've gone too far.

The path climbs, passing a bench on the right with fine views towards the Bristol Channel, before snaking its way up to reach a stone archway. Go through, up steps and along the path as it twists

DUNSTER AND CONYGAR TOWER

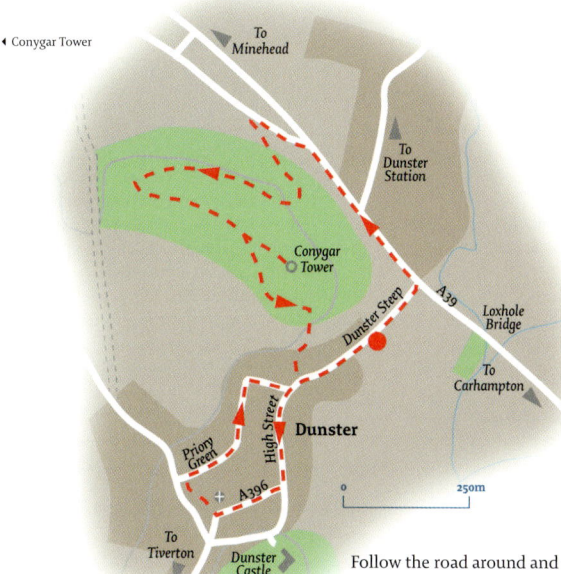

◀ Conygar Tower

upwards. Soon you'll reach the imposing Conygar Tower, a three-storey folly built atop this wooded hill.

Retrace your steps to the first wide turning on the left. Take this path, going straight down. It bends left and continues with glimpses of Dunster High Street on the right through trees. At a signpost, turn right for Dunster, passing through a kissing gate. On reaching the road, turn right and walk into the village, passing the historic Yarn Market with stunning Dunster Castle in view, too.

Follow the road around and through traffic lights. At a wrought-iron gate on the right, explore Dunster Village Gardens which, during the 16th century, were the castle's kitchen garden before falling into disuse. Fortunately, they've been restored.

Further on, turn right and walk through the church grounds. Exit at the back of the church onto Priory Green. Turn right, following the road through an archway and passing a dovecote on the left. Although unclear when this was built, records refer to repairs in the 18th and 19th centuries.

The road eventually joins Dunster Steep again. Turn left and return to the car park.

Grabbist Hill and Dunster

Distance 13km **Time** 3 hours 30
Terrain level walking with a steep climb up Grabbist Hill **Map** OS Explorer OL9
Access buses to Minehead from Taunton, Exmoor Coaster bus from Porlock and Lynmouth and trains to Minehead on the West Somerset Railway; roadside parking on Parkhouse Road

Heather-covered Grabbist Hill is said to be the 'purple-headed mountain' which inspired the Anglican hymn 'All Things Bright and Beautiful', first published by Cecil Frances Alexander in 1848. Although there are other claimants in Wales and Ireland it is hard to dispute Grabbist Hill's claim on a fine day. This ridge walk along the hill from Minehead to Dunster is never crowded and offers fine views.

Start at the top of Parkhouse Road and turn right onto Periton Road. After 180m, take a track on the left opposite Periton Lane, signed for Wootton Common.

At another signpost, take the path on the left, climbing into the trees. Follow it for a while until it is joined by a track on the right. Carry straight on, ignoring paths on the left and following the sign for Wootton Courtenay. This is the walk's steepest section. At the top, where the path levels out, bear left by a blue-capped post. Along the hill's ridge, you're treading the Macmillan Way West.

Ignoring paths on either side, continue along the hilltop in an easterly direction. On a clear day, you can see miles up the coast with the small Bristol Channel islands of Steep Holm and Flat Holm visible in the distance.

Carry on for Dunster, soon following the sign for the bridleway to Grabbist Hill. At the next fork, keep right.

GRABBIST HILL AND DUNSTER

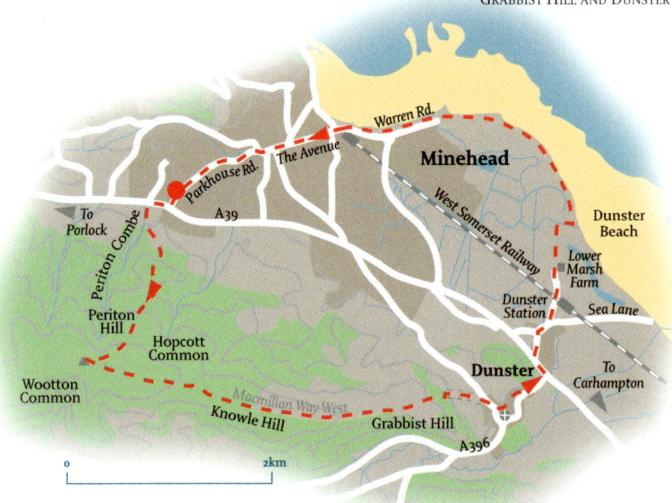

Where the path splits three ways, carry straight on along the hilltop. As the route descends, head straight on at the sign, passing a metal National Trust sign for Grabbist Hill on the right.

The path runs right of a field boundary. At the next sign, turn left for Dunster to follow the path as it drops steadily to another sign, indicating Dunster via Conduit Lane. The path reaches a large gate. Go through this onto Conduit Lane, which can be wet and muddy. Where the lane joins a road, turn right before going left opposite a school onto Priory Green.

After a stone archway, this pretty lane continues past a medieval dovecote and eventually reaches a main road, Dunster Steep. Turn left and walk down to traffic lights at a major road junction. Go under the subway, turning left upon emerging.

At Laundry Cottage, turn right down Marsh Lane.

When you reach a junction at a left bend, turn right for Dunster Station, part of the West Somerset Railway which runs from Minehead to Bishops Lydeard. Ignore Sea Lane as you continue, passing the station and later the entrance to Lower Marsh Farm and a footpath sign.

Once past the Old Manor, you go through five gates onto a track. At the end, turn right to head to a golf course and beach. A sign indicates the England Coast Path for Minehead, with the remains of a pebble-built war hut close by. Turn left and follow the path or beach to Minehead seafront. At the Jubilee Café, cross to the leafy Avenue and follow this to the Queen Anne statue and Park Street. Parkhouse Road is off Park Street.

◂ Looking up the coast to Blue Anchor and beyond

Bossington Hill and Selworthy

Distance 8km **Time** 2 hours
Terrain steep path up Selworthy Combe at the end of the walk **Map** OS Explorer OL9
Access car park at the end of Hill Road to the northwest of Minehead

Moorland, woodland, headlands, coastline, combes, picturesque villages and cream teas – this walk has it all. After heading out towards Hurlstone Point, the route sweeps around the hillside then descends to Allerford, a village mentioned in the Domesday Book, and continues to charming Selworthy.

From the car park, walk along the wide path heading towards the cairn atop Bossington Hill. After around five minutes, a track joins from the right and another soon after, but continue until you reach a signpost. Where a path drops to the left to Lynch Combe, go straight on, following the acorn sign.

As you progress, there are beautiful views across to the South Wales coast, down the undulating rocky coastline and over the rural landscape towards Dunkery Beacon, Exmoor's highest point.

The path gradually descends to a signpost where you bear left for the Coast Path to Bossington. The path drops further down the hill to another sign, close to a bench. Head for Lynch Combe. There are fine views of pebbly Bossington Beach and Porlock Bay as you walk around the hill.

After weaving around steep-sided Church Combe and through Allerford Plantation, you come to a junction of paths. Veer right for Allerford, passing through a gate and following a sign for St Agnes' Fountain, Allerford and Bossington. Drop down through the woods, ignoring tracks running back up the hill.

At a junction offering six routes, you've arrived at Agnes' Fountain. The trickling fountain has no saintly connection; it was named after the youngest daughter of Sir

◀ Porlock Bay

Thomas Acland who owned much land in the area.

Take the route for Allerford, continuing through the woods. At the next junction, pick the middle of the three options and descend to two gates. Passing through both, cross a field and through another gate to a narrow road marking your arrival in Allerford. Turn right and cross the picturesque packhorse bridge to explore this beautiful village.

To continue, retrace your steps over the bridge and up the narrow road, bending right. At thatched Jasmine Cottage on the left, keep ahead for Selworthy, joining a stony track edged by tall hedgerows. On entering Selworthy, you join a tarmac road and pass farm buildings before coming to another road. Turn left.

After the public toilets, look for a gate immediately on your left. Enter and walk up to National Trust-owned Selworthy Green, a picturesque setting with a cluster of lemon-painted thatched cottages, built in 1828 as almshouses for retired staff from the Holnicote Estate. The thatched Periwinkle Cottage Tea Rooms are irresistible and there are few places better in England to enjoy a clotted cream tea.

Follow the path up past the National Trust shop and through the gate at the war memorial. It's worth visiting the white lime-washed 14th-century Selworthy All Saints Church before returning to the memorial and turning uphill on the track for Selworthy Beacon.

The path leads into Selworthy Combe. At another signpost, keep right, continuing in the direction of the beacon. You need to branch left at the next sign.

Before long, the path emerges from the woods and skirts the trees. Just before reaching a road, turn left to the Wind and Weather Hut, erected in remembrance of Sir Thomas Acland in 1878. Follow the Easy Access Path back to the car park.

Woodcombe and North Hill

Distance 5.25km **Time** 1 hour 30
Terrain steep in places, especially after Wydon Farm and starting the descent into Woodcombe **Map** OS Explorer OL9
Access roadside parking in Bratton Lane

This walk begins in Woodcombe on the western edge of Minehead and aims for the tiny hamlet of Bratton before cutting up over fields onto North Hill. The return takes you down through quiet woodland.

Bratton Lane takes you west out of Woodcombe all the way to a junction. Here, head straight on in the direction of Hindon and Wydon Farms before turning right at the no-through road sign, near Bratton Court Farm.

Follow the footpath for Woodcombe. The path cuts between two fields, rising to a gate. Go through this and keep left, now turning away from Woodcombe. Pass through another gate and keep left for Wydon Farm. Follow the path, which runs alongside the fence, to the farm. Look out for a footpath sign for North Hill.

Go through a gate and cross a field to another gate. Turn left and follow the boundary. Soon, you'll enter a field where the views back towards Dunster, the village of Blue Anchor and the West Somerset coastline are stunning.

On entering another gate, walk up the edge of the field and turn sharp right at a sign where the track is now deep-rutted and the gradient increases.

The track eventually reaches a metal gate. Go through, turn immediately left and you'll reach Hill Road. Cross and walk ahead to a crossroads of paths. Head down to the field boundary, turning right towards Minehead with views of the Bristol Channel and Welsh coast beyond.

◀ Wydon Farm

Go through a wooden gate and straight on, marked by the acorn symbol. At the next sign, where a path joins on the left, look for a narrow path immediately on your right. Wending its way through heather and gorse, it soon meets Hill Road again.

Cross the road and follow the path for Woodcombe. It is extremely steep as it winds down into the valley. Ignore signs indicating Bratton and Moor Wood.

Eventually, the path turns into a tarmac lane. With a brook on your left, walk down the lane – soon houses will edge both sides. The lane bends left before a junction with a sign for Higher Orchard. Turn right. At the next junction, you'll be back on Bratton Lane.

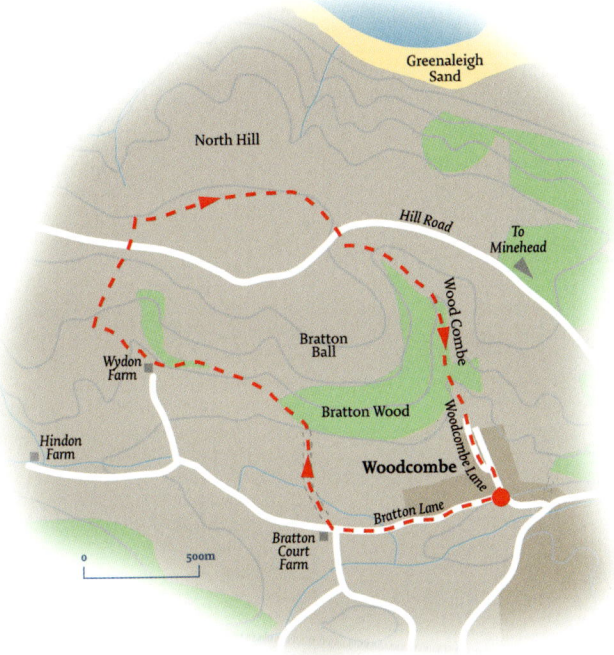

MINEHEAD AND THE BRENDON HILLS

Dunster and Bat's Castle

Distance 7.25km **Time** 2 hours
Terrain no particular difficulties, although there is a gradual climb through woods to Gallox Hill
Map OS Explorer OL9 **Access** buses to Dunster from Taunton, and Exmoor Coaster bus from Lynmouth, Porlock and Minehead; car park in Park Street, Dunster

From the pretty cobbled village of Dunster, this walk rises above woodland to Gallox Hill and the remains of an Iron Age hillfort before sweeping back around via fields and a deer park to the start.

From the car park, turn left and cross the Grade I-listed Gallox Bridge, soon picking up a sign for Bat's Castle and Carhampton. At a junction of paths, follow the middle track into Dunster Woodland, heading for Bat's Castle.

The path climbs through the forest before splitting: keep left to continue your ascent. At large wooden gates on the left, go through and climb up the track. Leaving the trees behind, the grassy path levels off before twisting and dropping.

Approaching the summit, aim for the bench just before the castle – or what remains of the 6th-century BC Iron Age hillfort. The ditch and bank are all that have survived of this circular enclosure, but it's an impressive site with panoramic views across the Bristol Channel to South Wales and back towards Dunkery Beacon.

Keep straight ahead, ignoring paths either side. At a large gate, go through, turn right and then immediately left for Withycombe Hill.

Soon, you'll reach another gate. After entering, trees fringe the path's left side, running along Withycombe Hill, with fine views across to Black Hill and wooded Croydon Hill.

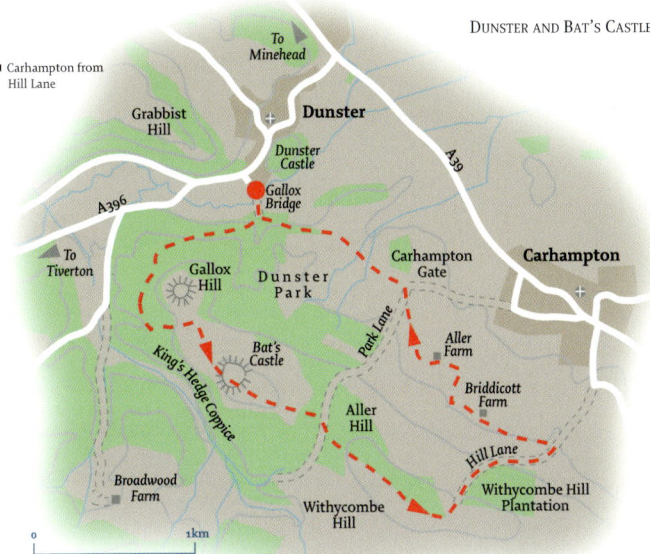

◀ Carhampton from Hill Lane

At the next sign, head straight on, marked for Hill Lane, Carhampton, followed shortly by another sign for Carhampton. The path drops. As the route leaves the trees behind, your route is bordered by fields. Look for a sign high up and turn left for Dunster via Aller Farm.

First, the footpath takes you through Briddicott Farm and out the other side. Go through a gate, heading diagonally to the right across a field to another gate and yellow-capped post. Go through this and keep left, close to the hedge.

At another gate, on the left where you'll see a yellow waymark, enter the field, keeping left of the hedge with Aller Farm ahead. Go through a gate, turning immediately left. The track now skirts Aller Farm, splitting opposite a metal gate. Carry on ahead, passing a hay barn.

Keep right where the track starts to climb and eventually enter a field. Cross the field in a diagonal direction to the next waymark. At a signpost for Dunster, go through the high Carhampton Gate, one of the official entrances into the medieval deer park. Before the A39 road was constructed, this was the main route into Dunster.

Continue to Dunster, just over 1km away. Head down over a field, keeping to the right-hand boundary, with the magnificent National Trust-owned Dunster Castle ahead. Go through a kissing gate alongside a metal one, and carry on. Soon the outskirts of Dunster appear and the route swings around to the thatched cottages and car park.

Lynmouth was once described by Thomas Gainsborough as 'the most delightful place for a landscape painter this country can boast'. The North Exmoor coast undoubtedly has spectacular coastal views and these feature in many of the walks in this chapter, while other routes explore some of the national park's more remote inland corners.

Highlights of this part of the Exmoor coast include the fascinating Valley of Rocks, a dry valley noted for its unusual geology, landscape features and feral goat population, and the Glen Lyn Gorge where peaceful riverside walks can be enjoyed.

In contrast, the upland plateau known as The Chains is cloaked in blanket bog which can be more than a metre thick; yet a walk here is a challenge many are glad they rose to. A focal point for walks around here is Pinkery Pond, a great place for a picnic before continuing on your way. Due to its peat base, the waters appear dark and secretive but, in truth, this is a lovely spot.

The desolate Hoar Oak Valley can similarly be a foreboding place in the wrong weather, but on a fine clear day there are few better places in which to escape the modern world.

Exe Head and West Exmoor

1. **Pinkery Pond and Mole's Chamber** 76
   Head onto the high moors to a remote 'pond' that's really a man-made lake

2. **Brendon Two Gates to Badgworthy** 78
   Explore the remains of a medieval farming village 'at the head of a deep green valley'

3. **Exe Head and Hoar Oak Cottage** 80
   An evocative and remote ruin is the highlight of this quiet valley walk

4. **Hoar Oak Valley to Pinkery Pond** 82
   Stretch your legs on this longer exploration of a high boggy plateau

5. **Watersmeet from Lynmouth** 84
   Follow the river inland from a coastal village to a perfectly-sited National Trust tea garden

6. **Lynmouth to Countisbury** 86
   Take the riverside path along the East Lyn before heading to a former West Saxon stronghold

7. **The Valley of Rocks** 88
   A rewarding loop from Lynton to a great viewpoint and a popular area full of geological interest

8. **Countisbury circular** 90
   This circuit of heathland takes in a lookout over the rocky headland

9. **Hunter's Inn and Martinhoe** 92
   Walk up a steep-sided valley to pick up the Coast Path for stunning views

10. **Trentishoe Down and Holdstone Hill** 94
    Enjoy great views before hitting the glorious Coast Path

Pinkery Pond and Mole's Chamber

Distance 9km **Time** 2 hours 30
Terrain mainly flat other than a couple of short climbs; can be very boggy so best walked after a long dry spell, preferably in summer **Map** OS Explorer OL9
Access lay-by on the right of the B3358, 5km from Simonsbath

This walk takes in a remote corner of Exmoor; choose your day well because the area around The Chains can be extremely boggy. Despite the forbidding landscape, there was once a 'disreputable hostelry' near Mole's Chamber where smuggled brandy could be found. Whether or not the unfortunate Rev Mole who fell from his horse and drowned here in 1752 had enjoyed too much of it before meeting his boggy end is not known.

From the lay-by, look for a wooden gate and follow the bridleway sign to The Chains. This segment of the walk is along the Macmillan Way West and ventures up over a field, with a boundary on your right. It's a steady climb to a wire fence. Go through a gate and up over Goat Hill to another five-bar gate. Once through, follow the grassy path across the field. You'll notice another grass track crossing your path, but continue ahead; the route is periodically marked by splashes of blue on posts.

Crossing open land, you reach a gate and sign at a boundary where you turn left to head towards Pinkery Pond, or you can choose to detour to the 487m-high summit of Chains Barrow before retracing your steps to this point. From here, you can walk either side of the boundary, but the southern side is easiest. You eventually go through a gate, just as the terrain begins to drop away on reaching the pond, the ideal spot for a rest.

Situated 440m above sea level, the pond was built just under 200 years ago for the Midlands industrialist John Knight.

PINKERY POND AND MOLE'S CHAMBER

Created by building a dam across the River Barle, it is thought the pond was part of an ambitious but failed irrigation system.

Once you're fully refreshed, walk to the western side of the pond in the direction of Woodbarrow Gate. Beyond a gate, the path crosses open land.

You gradually approach a field boundary on the right and a gate in the corner. Turn left, keeping within the field, signed for the B3358. You've now joined the Tarka Trail, running south across Broad Mead. Head down to a boundary which no longer has a gate. The track isn't the most discernible. To your left stands the solitary wind turbine at Pinkery Centre for Outdoor Learning, a former Victorian farmstead now owned by the Exmoor National Park Authority.

The path hugs the right-hand boundary until it reaches a road. Cross the B3358 and join the path opposite, heading for Mole's Chamber. The track climbs to a signpost. Continue for Mole's Chamber, keeping the fence on your right. At the next sign, by a field boundary, continue on the bridleway.

On reaching a pair of gates, take the right-hand option and go through the next gate. Follow the path around to the head of Lew Combe and pass the Sloley Stone, an inscribed boundary stone. Turn left for the bog known as Mole's Chamber.

The path crosses a stream and makes its way to a small wooden gate. Enter and follow the narrow path running up by the wire fence before twisting away and picking up the blue-capped waymarks.

The route runs above the marshy valley of Great Vintcombe. To your left, you'll spot the B3358 and the lay-by at the start. Eventually, a wider track joins from the right. Turn left and walk down through a five-bar gate. At the next gate, where you join a concrete track, turn left and go down the hill, crossing a bridge. At the road, turn left to reach the start point.

◆ Pinkery Pond

Brendon Two Gates to Badgworthy

Distance 8.25km **Time** 2 hours 30
Terrain some steep gradients but a relatively easy walk **Map** OS Explorer OL9
Access parking in lay-by south of the cattle grid at Brendon Two Gates

This route begins north of the village of Simonsbath at Brendon Two Gates and heads east across a wild and remote landscape to visit the remains of a medieval farming village. It is thought that the isolated and abandoned ruins, hidden away high on the moor, inspired R D Blackmore's depiction of the hideout of the troublesome Doone family and for a time it became a place of pilgrimage for fans of his novel.

From the lay-by, cross the cattle grid and look for an unmarked, slightly undefined grassy path on the right. Take this, before veering left to cross Open Access Land in the direction of the stone memorial on the horizon.

This is the Maclaren Memorial, a granite pillar close to Hoccombe Hill's summit. It was erected in memory of the selfless Colonel Maclaren, who was killed here in 1941 when he threw himself onto a faulty prototype explosive device during a weapons demonstration for government officials and fellow officers.

Turn back, facing the way you came, and head in the direction of the plantation that is just visible on a distant ridge. You'll need to pick up the grassy track again, after which you turn left and head towards a gate within a field boundary in the distance. The path becomes a little more distinguishable as you head towards the gate.

Don't go through the gate. Instead, turn right and follow the field boundary down to Hoccombe Water, passing the stone remains of a ruined building. Continue down to the stream. Go through the gate, turn left and follow the stream and the

Brendon Two Gates to Badgworthy

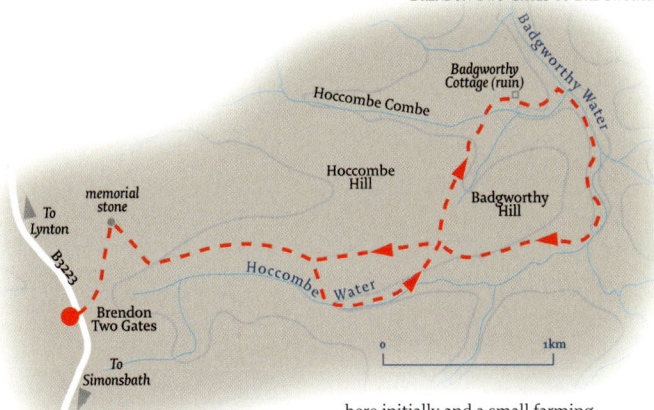

stone wall, which marked the boundary of the former Royal Forest of Exmoor, to another gate on the left. Go through and turn right, heading diagonally up to meet the grassy track you'll spot from the gate.

The path climbs. Where a broad track crosses near the top of the hill, carry on ahead. The route descends to the bottom of Hoccombe Hill, where you bear left. At a sign, walk through the gap in the wall and cross the stream.

On the other side, walk up to the ruins of what was once Badgworthy Cottage before continuing down the valley, following the path on your right.

At a split, bear left towards Malmsmead. After about 50m, turn right at the next junction, signed for Manor Allotment. Amongst ferns and grass, you might be able to make out the foundations of the medieval village of Badgworthy.

Established by the Knights Hospitallers in the 12th century, there was a chapel here initially and a small farming community which is thought to have survived to the 14th century. Cheaper rents elsewhere, probably following the Black Death, led the farmers to leave their houses to be reclaimed by nature. R D Blackmore knew this spot, 'at the head of a deep green valley', very well and it is easy to see how he found inspiration in the ruins and wild landscape here.

Head down the footpath to a large gate and small bridge over a stream. Cross over and head south, keeping Badgworthy Water on your left as you walk around the base of Badgworthy Hill. Soon you'll notice a gate, ford and footbridge over the stream on your left. Your route, however, remains on the right side of the water with the path climbing the hillside.

What begins as a stony path becomes a broad grassy track. When you reach a junction of tracks which you crossed earlier, carry straight on, through a gate and eventually back to the lay-by on the B3223 at the start.

◀ Maclaren Memorial

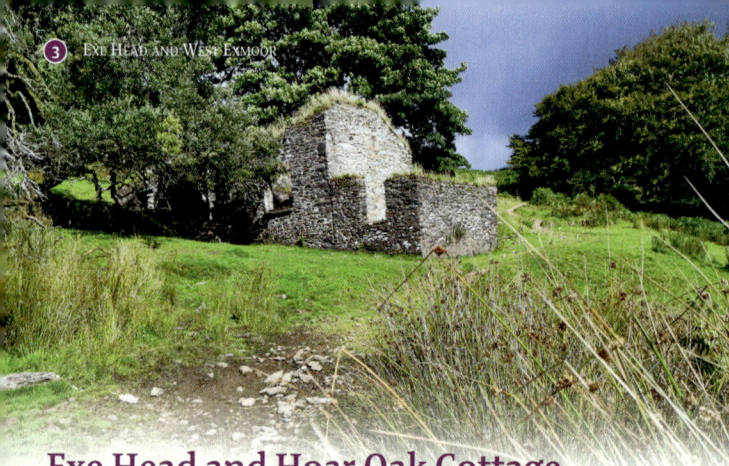

Exe Head and Hoar Oak Cottage

Distance 5.75km **Time** 2 hours
Terrain straightforward walk
Map OS Explorer OL9 **Access** lay-by just to the north of Prayway Head on B3223, outside Simonsbath

This straightforward walk visits the source of the River Exe, which runs south for more than 90km to the south coast, as well as a tranquil valley and the wonderfully preserved ruin of Hoar Oak Cottage, once home to a unique community of hardy Scots.

Go through the gate at the lay-by, signed for Exe Head, turn right and follow the path with the bridleway marker.

After a few metres, go through another gate. Here, you have two choices. You'll notice an unmarked route heading across the field in a northwesterly direction. The signed route turns immediately left, however, running alongside the boundary on the left.

Taking this option, walk up over the field. At a signpost where the field boundary ends, head in the direction of Exe Head, crossing Dure Down on the Two Moors Way, the long-distance trail established in 1976 linking Dartmoor with Exmoor.

Pick your way across and down to a signpost at a gate and a junction of paths known as Exe Head, the source of the River Exe. Head for Hoar Oak, continuing not only on the Two Moors Way but now also the Tarka Trail, a 290km route crossing North Devon and Exmoor.

When you meet a slight track on your right at a bend, ignore it and carry on down into the deep-sided valley. Cross the stream at the point where it meets the steep-sided Long Chains Combe.

Continue, with the ruins of an enclosure up on the left, off the path. Soon, you'll pass a scattering of large stones on the other side of the valley on

Exe Head and Hoar Oak Cottage

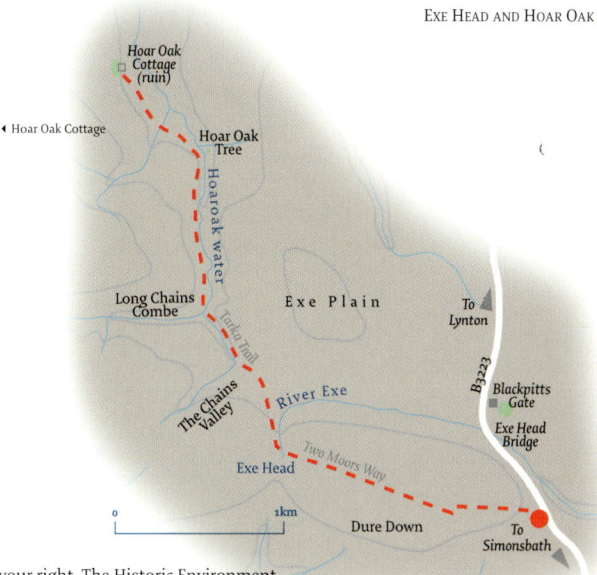

◀ Hoar Oak Cottage

your right. The Historic Environment Record for Exmoor National Park suggests that the site of a stone working area on the east floodplain of Hoaroak Water, including 'the presence of about a dozen large stone slabs, drilled for use as gateposts', may have been associated with the development of the enclosure system in the early 19th century.

Further along, surrounded by a wooden fence, is the Hoar Oak Tree. Apparently, an oak has stood here for years, marking the boundary between the Royal Forest of Exmoor and Brendon Common.

As the path bends left, you approach a signpost at two gates. Go through the bigger gate, signed for Stock Common.

The tussocky path crosses a stream and goes through a gate on the other side of the water. Where the path splits, go left up to the conserved ruin of Hoar Oak Cottage. In 1841, Frederick Knight, who owned more than 16,000 acres of Exmoor, decided to establish year-round 'sheep ranching' and transported 15,000 tough Blackface and Cheviot sheep, as well as 20 Scottish shepherds and their families from around Lanark and Dumfries in the Scottish Lowlands, to the area. The cottage became home to four of the families, and other farmhouses were built up in the hills to accommodate the rest.

Spend time at the cottage admiring this wild region and the fortitude of the people who lived and worked in this remote spot before retracing your steps.

Hoar Oak Valley to Pinkery Pond

Distance 12.75km **Time** 4 hours 30
Terrain no specific challenges in terms of ascent and descent, but areas of this walk can get boggy after wet weather so it is best walked during a dry spell and in good visibility **Map** OS Explorer OL9
Access lay-by just north of Prayway Head on the B3223, outside Simonsbath

This route is an extension of the preceding walk to the remote Hoar Oak Cottage and heads around remote parts of The Chains, the high northwest plateau, before visiting Pinkery Pond on the way back to Exe Head. A Geological Conservation Area, the plateau is nationally important and transitions from being an ancient semi-natural woodland through upland heath to blanket mire. If you like bog, you'll love this walk.

From the ruin of Hoar Oak Cottage (see previous walk), follow the path into a field and up over to the remains of an old gate flagged with a blue bridleway mark. You now head in a largely northwesterly direction across Furzehill Common.

This stretch of the walk can be boggy after wet weather and the path is indiscernible in places so just pick your way across, looking out for a public bridleway marker post. You also pass a pile of stones. Eventually, the path leads towards a gate where two boundaries meet. Go through this and walk in the direction of North Furzehill and Stock Common, crossing three fields.

At the end of the third, don't go through the gate but instead turn left towards Shallowford and through a nearby gate, marked with bridleway blue.

The path runs close to the tree-lined boundary to meet a gate. Go through this and down the stony track to a narrow road. Turn left. After the road bends right, head for North Furzehill and Shallowford at a sign on your right, followed shortly after by a bridleway sign for Shallowford.

HOAR OAK VALLEY TO PINKERY POND

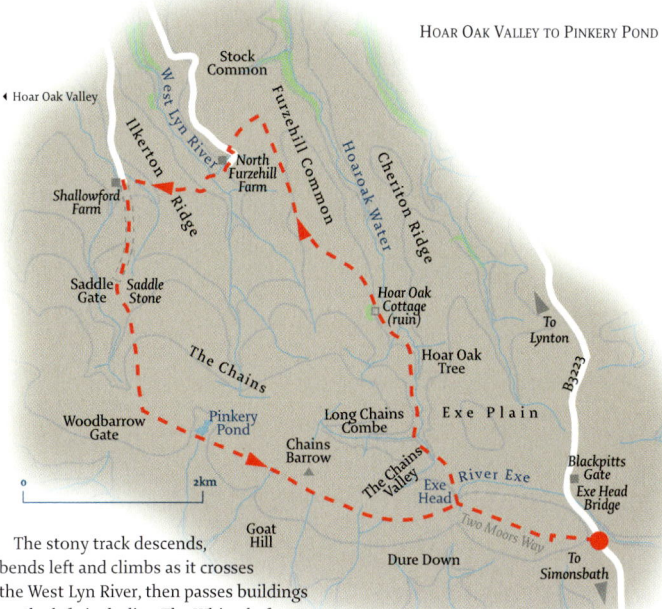

The stony track descends, bends left and climbs as it crosses the West Lyn River, then passes buildings on the left, including The Whim, before a gate. Go through this, turning left and then immediately right. There are no signs – it's just a case of making your way westwards across Ilkerton Ridge through rough grass.

Eventually, you'll see a cottage and old barn alongside fields – this is Shallowford Farm. Aim for these buildings and, when you get to the farm, turn left and walk up the unclassified road to Saddle Gate on a steady climb.

Saddle Stone is situated to the left of Saddle Gate. This boundary stone marked the division between Devon and Somerset and the edge of Exmoor Forest.

After passing through a gate, the path climbs and then crosses The Chains. There are no markers here and it can be boggy. In a while, you'll see a field boundary and signpost ahead – this is Woodbarrow Gate.

Turn in the direction of Exe Head and walk across to a field boundary and gate. Go through and down to Pinkery Pond.

Leaving the pond, follow the path for Exe Head running along a boundary. When you meet two gates on the right, go through the second and turn left, keeping close to the boundary. It's an easier route than on the other side.

Keep to the southern side of the boundary all the way back to Exe Head. From here, follow the instructions on the previous walk to return to the lay-by.

Watersmeet from Lynmouth

Distance 6km **Time** 1 hour 30
Terrain straightforward walk
Map OS Explorer OL9 **Access** Exmoor Coaster bus to Lynmouth from Watchet, Minehead and Porlock; Lower Lyndale car park, Lynmouth

This popular walk up Glen Lyn Gorge follows the fast-flowing East Lyn River from the picturesque coastal village of Lynmouth to where it meets Hoar Oak Water, the setting for a tea garden not to be missed (so long as you visit between spring and October). Look out for heron fishing in some of the quieter spots and deeper pools along the river. If you are very lucky you might also spot an otter.

From the car park, head east, following the river away from the sea. Cross the footbridge, turn right and walk along the road. At the end of the street, you'll pick up the footpath sign for Watersmeet.

Arriving at a wooden footbridge, don't cross the river but carry straight on. The path follows the river, which is on your right, and when you reach the Arnold's Linhay signpost, bear left and take the Woodland Walk to Watersmeet which begins with a bit of a climb.

At the next sign, drop down on the path for Watersmeet, continuing on the Woodland Walk all the way to Watersmeet House. Sitting at the bottom of a deep gorge at the confluence of the East Lyn River and Hoar Oak Water, the National Trust property was built as a fishing lodge in 1832 and has been home to a popular tea garden for more than 100 years.

Adjoining the property is the Watersmeet SSSI (Site of Special Scientific Interest) which contains an extensive area of ancient oak woodland, as well as a very

◀ Watersmeet House

rare species of whitebeam tree which has only been found to grow in this area.

Leaving Watersmeet House, cross the river at the wooden footbridge and then a smaller bridge.

Follow the stony footpath up an incline and when the path bends left, go right, dropping back down to the riverside.

Don't cross a stone bridge. Carry on and, at a signpost, continue on the permitted footpath for Lynmouth. Take care, especially when the path is wet, because you're right alongside the river.

Soon, you'll reach Lynrock Fountain, marking the spot where the Lynrock Mineral Water factory opened in 1911. Here, mineral water was bottled and ginger beer made until its closure in 1939. Sadly, most of the abandoned factory was washed away during the Lynmouth Disaster of 1952, a devastating flood which claimed the lives of 34 local people. Boulders left by the floodwater can still be seen along the banks of the river towards Lynmouth.

Eventually, you'll cross the East Lyn River via a wooden bridge. Walk up to a signpost you'll recognise from your outward journey. From here, follow the path back to Lynmouth.

Lynmouth to Countisbury

Distance 4.75km **Time** 1 hour 30
Terrain steep climb through Wester Wood, otherwise relatively straightforward
Map OS Explorer OL9 **Access** Exmoor Coaster bus to Lynmouth from Watchet, Minehead and Porlock; Lower Lyndale car park, Lynmouth

This varied walk follows the East Lyn River east along Glen Lyn Gorge from the picturesque coastal village of Lynmouth before cutting up through Wester Wood to the tiny hilltop village of Countisbury, a former West Saxon stronghold. The route returns via the scenic South West Coast Path.

From Lower Lyndale car park, walk in an easterly direction, following the river away from the sea. Cross the footbridge, turning right and walking along the road. Reaching the end of the street, you'll pick up a footpath sign for Watersmeet.

At a wooden footbridge, don't cross the river; instead carry straight on. The path follows the river, which is on your right. When you reach the Arnold's Linhay signpost, bear left and take the Woodland Walk towards Watersmeet.

Arnold's Linhay comprises a series of enclosures on the south-facing slope of Wind Hill, including at least five grassed-over crossbanks with the remains of walls.

At the next signpost, bear left uphill to Countisbury. The path winds its way up through the trees until you reach a signpost by a bench. Continue on the route for Countisbury.

Although the exact location is not

◀ The path to Countisbury

known, the Battle of Cynuit between the West Saxons and Vikings probably took place on the hillside here in 878. The Vikings, led by Ubba, brother of Ivan the Boneless and Halfdan Ragnarsson, sailed from Dyfred and landed nearby with 23 ships and 1200 men. The West Saxons unexpectedly came down from their fort on Wind Hill, however, and routed the larger force, killing Ubba and capturing their fabled flag of war, the 'Raven banner'. This was good news for Alfred the Great who was struggling to fight off the Vikings in the marshes of Somerset at the time.

Eventually, you go through a gate and cross the A39 to another gate slightly to the west. (Countisbury is to the east.) Go through the gate, signed for the Coast Path to Lynmouth, and climb up to go through a further gate.

Walk up over the field, keeping close to the right-hand field boundary. At the next sign, ignore the finger pointing left to Lynmouth. Instead, go through the gate on your right and at the next sign turn left to join the South West Coast Path.

From here, simply follow the path along the dramatic coastline to return to Lynmouth.

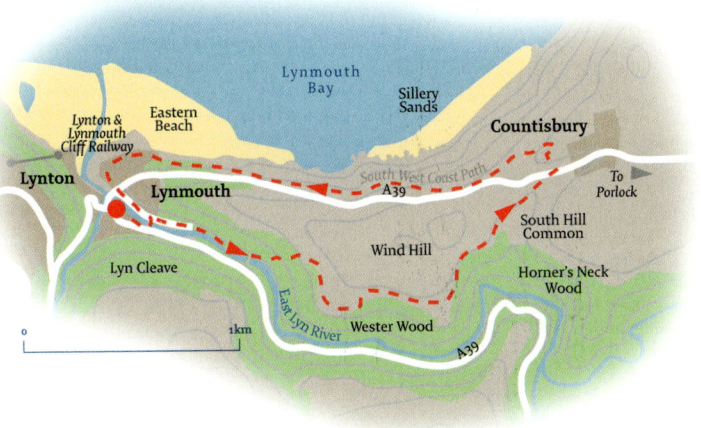

The Valley of Rocks

Distance 3.5km **Time** 1 hour 30 **Terrain** easy walk but care needed along the Coast Path approaching the Valley of Rocks **Map** OS Explorer OL9 **Access** car park in Lynton or roadside parking

This walk begins in the hilltop village of Lynton and takes you into a magical corner of Exmoor. A popular tourist attraction with an evocative name, the Valley of Rocks is a seemingly secret world, tucked away under the shelter of surrounding hills just a stone's throw from Lynton.

At the Parish Church of St Mary the Virgin, turn into the no-through road of North Walk Hill and continue in the direction of the Valley of Rocks.

Pass North Walk House and the Chough's Nest Hotel on the narrow road which becomes a tarmac path, running around a steep wooded hillside. On the right, there is soon a severe drop to the Bristol Channel.

The path twists around the coast to a split. For a short detour, turn left, signed for Lynton and Holler Day Hill. On the right, above seats, is a fine vantage point. Look out for the local feral goats which can be seen roaming freely or balancing precariously on jagged outcrops.

Returning to the signpost, turn left back onto the Coast Path to explore the Valley of Rocks. This dry valley contains some of the oldest Devonian rocks in north Devon and is highly fossiliferous.

◀ Valley of Rocks

The well-travelled Romantic poets Samuel Taylor Coleridge and William Wordsworth found inspiration here, as of course did R D Blackmore, who made this the setting for part of *Lorna Doone*.

After enjoying the rocks, head up the road towards a car park and keep an eye out for Mother Meldrum's Tea Garden (seasonal opening). Mother Meldrum was the witch-cum-soothsayer in *Lorna Doone* and the character is said to be based on one Aggie Norman, a local woman with a reputation as a healer who lived for part of the year in the valley.

Continue up the road and take the grassy path signed for Lynton opposite the spectacularly-set Lynton and Lynmouth Cricket Club.

The path climbs to a gate and trees before levelling out. Soon, you pass a cemetery before the houses of Lynton come into view. Keep high where the path splits, with the left-hand route leading down to the cemetery.

Continue ahead on meeting a path for Lee Abbey on your right. Eventually, the path joins a narrow tarmac lane, known as Lydiate Lane or County Road.

Turn down the lane, marked for Lynton via the County Road, which drops steeply and bends left. Meeting a main road at Station Hill, on a sharp bend, continue down, passing a children's play area and bowling green on the left. Follow the road around into Crossmead. At the end of the road, turn right onto Lee Road, where Lynton's shops begin, and you soon arrive at the car park.

Countisbury circular

Distance 3.25km **Time** 1 hour
Terrain busy road section at the start, otherwise easy going with two short steep sections **Map** OS Explorer OL9
Access car park off Countisbury Hill on the A39

This short walk, circling the pretty hamlet of Countisbury, can be enjoyed any time of day, but the sunset from The Foreland, a rocky headland managed by the National Trust, and the most northerly point along this stretch of coast, is well worth waiting for.

From the car park, turn right onto the A39. Take care because you must negotiate a stretch of this busy road. Walk down, passing a cattle grid and Countisbury roadsign before turning left onto a footpath for Watersmeet, just short of a sharp bend.

Go through the gate and walk up the grassy track, passing through two more gates before descending over a field. Look for a yellow-capped post in a gap between gorse bushes. Carry on down and through a gate, turning right onto Winston's Path. Continue up a stepped section of the

footpath and through another gate before following it around the hillside. There are fine views before you eventually drop down to a small pond. Turn left to walk around the pond and up a grassy path, beside a stone wall, to a gate by the A39.

Cross the road and join another path opposite, signed as a permitted footpath and the Coast Path for Lynmouth. Continue up, passing through another wooden gate. At the end of the stone wall on your right, the path turns right, signed for the Coast Path to Lynmouth. Go through the large five-bar gate.

At the following signpost, continue along the Coast Path with the next landmark being the communications tower on top of the headland. Before taking the path up to the tower, beginning by a wooden bench, carry on along the Coast Path which turns left and goes around the headland.

After around 70m you'll find a seat with one of England's best views. Similarly, a visit to the communications tower in summer offers beautiful sunsets and far-reaching coastal views.

On reaching the tower, head southeast downhill to reach a boundary. Turn left and follow the path alongside the boundary. Keep right at the fork and head back to the car park.

Hunter's Inn and Martinhoe

Distance 7.25km **Time** 1 hour 30
Terrain steep descent on road upon returning to Hunter's Inn
Map OS Explorer OL9 **Access** roadside parking near Hunter's Inn or in the National Trust car park

At the head of one of England's deepest valleys, the National Trust's charming Arts and Craft-style Hunter's Inn marks the start of this walk. Heading along the wooded Heddon Valley, the route takes in fine sea views on a spectacular coastal path before sweeping back to the inn via the hamlet of Martinhoe. If you are lucky, you may spot the UK's last surviving colonies of high brown fritillary butterflies on the bracken-covered hillsides in summer.

Facing Hunter's Inn, walk a few metres up the road on the right. As the road bends sharp right, continue straight ahead on a wide footpath marked as a public bridleway for Heddon's Mouth and a public footpath for Woody Bay.

Around 70m later, the path splits. Take the right-hand fork for Woody Bay, heading up through Road Wood. Down on your left, the River Heddon runs towards Heddon's Mouth.

The route climbs steadily through trees before bending around a steep combe, with Hill Brook running through it towards the Heddon. The path bends back at the head of the combe and sweeps to the right, with glorious sea views in both directions, including all the way to Foreland Point, near Lynmouth.

Look out for a wooden sign on your right, directing you to a viewpoint and Roman fortlet. It's a brief detour up a steep narrow path. The earthworks have a circumference of around 80m and were excavated in the 1960s.

Hunter's Inn and Martinhoe

◀ The South West Coast Path

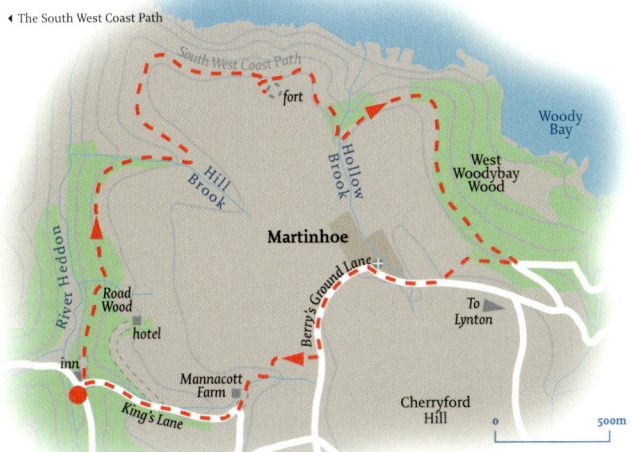

Retrace your steps to the main path and continue as it bends around another combe, this one containing Hollow Brook, and along the top of West Woodybay Wood. Go through the next gate and soon you'll see Woody Bay through the trees on your left.

Keep on the bridleway. When you reach a tarmac road on a sharp bend, follow the sign on the right, marked for Martinhoe Common. A little way up the path, ignore a route heading down on the right.

The path soon reaches a road which takes you into Martinhoe. Walk past buildings, including the lovely St Martin Church. Follow the road as it bends left by the postbox, continuing along what is known as Berry's Ground Lane, a narrow but quiet road.

Look for a cut in the right-hand hedge and a sign for Hunter's Inn. Go through a gate with a yellow-capped post.

Walk down the field, close to the right-hand boundary. At the next sign, head in the direction of Mannacott, bending left and dropping down the side of the field, canopied by hedgerows.

At the bottom of this steep rubbly path, go through a small gate, turning left and immediately right to follow a path along the edge of a brook. Soon, you'll go through two gates, the second positioned between two stone buildings at Mannacott Farm.

With the farmhouse in front, take the partly tarmacked track on the left, climbing to a road on an exceedingly sharp bend. Turn right and walk back down to Hunter's Inn.

10 EXE HEAD AND WEST EXMOOR

Trentishoe Down and Holdstone Hill

Distance 7km **Time** 2 hours
Terrain mostly easy walking but a few climbs, especially the very steep ascent from Ladies' Mile to Trentishoe Lane and a steady climb up Holdstone Hill
Map OS Explorer OL9 **Access** off-road car park to the southeast of Holdstone Hill: entrance has a blue metal height barrier

A walk over the open Trentishoe Down, where the 324m high point is crowned by two late Bronze Age round cairns. The route follows a path known as Ladies' Mile before climbing steeply and continuing westwards along the South West Coast Path, returning to the start over the summit of Holdstone Hill.

From the car park, turn left and walk up the road. On the right, the vast open heathland of Trentishoe Down contrasts with the undulating agricultural landscape beyond.

Walk past a bungalow, on the right. At two metal posts opposite another car park, turn onto a track. The wide path cuts across the down before dropping away.

Where the path forks at a small post emblazoned with an arrow, ignore the right-hand option and continue down. The narrow path is steep in places, particularly as it descends through trees to a much wider path known as Ladies' Mile, so called because it was used by women from Trentishoe Manor to reach the local church.

Turn left onto Ladies' Mile, a path bordered predominantly by silver birch, and carry on for some distance. At a

Trentishoe Down and Holdstone Hill

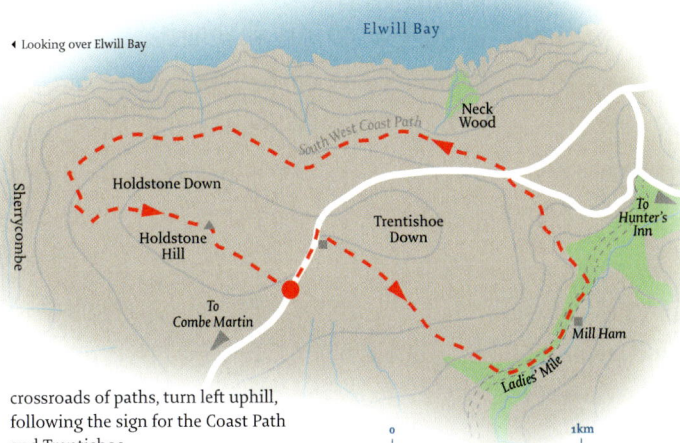

◀ Looking over Elwill Bay

crossroads of paths, turn left uphill, following the sign for the Coast Path and Trentishoe.

The path climbs to a road. Turn left to reach a roadsign at a junction, with a car park on the right. Enter the car park and take the track leading off in a northwesterly direction.

Paths join near a field entrance, but carry on, keeping close to the boundary on the right. Where the South West Coast Path joins on the right, carry on towards Combe Martin. The path soon bends left and climbs, with breathtaking views along the coast.

Continue on the Coast Path towards Combe Martin. Eventually, the path passes through a stone boundary cutting across your route. Carry on along the Coast Path with the impressive Great Hangman and Blackstone Point ahead.

As you approach the drop into Sherrycombe, the path turns sharp left and climbs before bending right, just as a minor path joins on the left. At a sign, turn left and climb in the County Road direction. Soon, you meet a crossroads of grassy paths. Turn left onto an unsigned path and begin your ascent onto Holdstone Hill. The path turns to the right at a tumbledown stone wall, then cuts between gorse and heather. Eventually, you reach the trig point and excavated cairns. There are more than 370 of these mounds recorded on Exmoor, mostly from the period 2400 to 1500BC and often covering multiple burials.

Leave the summit by the exit path on the right, nearest the trig point, and descend to the car park.

Index

Allerford	68	Leighland Chapel	58
Allotment, The	44	Liscombe	42
Anstey Gate	40	Lynmouth	84, 86
Badgworthy	78	Lynton	84, 86, 88
Barle Valley	52	Malmsmead	22
Bat's Castle	72	Martinhoe	92
Bossington Hill	68	Minehead	66
Brendon	22	Mole's Chamber	76
Brendon Two Gates	78	Nettlecombe	60
Broomstreet	14	North Hill	62, 70
Brushford	34	Nutscale Water	16
Butter Hill	90	Oare	12
Bye Common	46	Pinkery Pond	76, 82
Chains, The	76, 82	Porlock	16, 20
Chains Barrow	76	Porlock Hill	10
Conygar Tower	64	Prayway Head	54
Countisbury	20, 86, 90	Prescott	28
County Gate	22, 24	Punchbowl, The	44
Culbone Wood	20	Roadwater	58, 60
Doone Valley	22	Robber's Bridge	12
Dulverton	34, 36	Selworthy	68
Dunkery Beacon	30	Simonsbath	52, 54
Dunster	64, 66, 72	Sister's Fountain	24
East Lyn River	84, 86	Tarr Steps	42
Exe Head	54, 80, 82	Treborough	58
Exford	26, 28	Trentishoe Down	94
Foreland Point	20, 90	Valley of Rocks, The	88
Glen Lyn Gorge	84	Watersmeet House	84
Grabbist Hill	66	West Anstey Common	40
Haddon Hill	38	Wheal Eliza	52
Hawkridge	40	Wimbleball Lake	38
Heddon Valley	92	Winsford	44, 46
Hoar Oak Cottage	80, 82	Winsford Hill	42
Holdstone Hill	94	Withypool	48, 50
Horner	18	Withypool Hill	50
Hunter's Inn	92	Woodcombe	70
Landacre Bridge	48	Yenworthy	14